Bookdealing for Profit

BOOKDEALING
FOR
PROFIT

PAUL MINET

RICHARD
JOSEPH
PUBLISHERS LTD

Also by the author
Late Booking

First published 2000 by
Richard Joseph Publishers Ltd
Unit 2, Monks Walk
Farnham, Surrey GU9 8HT

Text set in 11/12pt Century Schoolbook
Printed and bound by MPG Books,
Victoria Square, Bodmin, Cornwall PL31 1EG

ISBN: 1 872699 70 7

Cover design by DP&D Design, Four Marks

CONTENTS

CONTENTS

PREFACE

This is a small introduction to a large field. Whilst it was being considered, a somewhat similar but vastly more detailed work was published on the same subject, but with a very different approach. Stuart Baldwin's *Beginner's Guide to Secondhand Bookselling* (Baldwin Books, September 1999 £24.00) beat my book into the market by months, partly because I started later, also because I have been extremely busy being president of the Antiquarian Booksellers' Association but mainly because of family circumstances in that I lost a daughter, a tragedy which, curiously enough, will also be the subject of a book to be published in June 2000 entitled *A Shadow in Tiger-Country* by my son-in-law.

During the delay caused by these problems, I have had time to think again about what this book is to be about. I have for almost thirty of my forty-five years in this trade been writing columns in various magazines about the secondhand book trade. Much of what I have written has been severely practical, but I have found that the articles which have excited the most comment have been those concerned with what might be called the *philosophy* of the business. My previous book on this trade, *Late Booking*, took the form of reminiscences of my first twenty-five years in the trade. It put a lot of people off going into bookselling, so I am told, an effect for which I make no apology. There is quite a lot written about the lifestyle of secondhand booksellers, but little about the high risks and the short life many dealers have in the trade.

Reading Mr Baldwin's estimable book, I came to the conclusion that he had covered the nuts and bolts of the trade fairly thoroughly and I commend his book. If it has one fault, it is not of his making: things are moving so quickly in this business that elements of his work are already out of date. Indeed, I received my own copy of his book somewhat late because two binders asked to bind his second batch of sheets went bankrupt before they could deliver. The major magazine in the American field, *AB Weekly*, has also bitten the dust since September last and the position of both major price lists, *Book Auction Records* and *American Book Prices Current*, has changed significantly. Finally, it almost goes without saying that his final section on the Internet also looks dated within six months of publication. None the less, there is much good solid matter in his pages, especially as regards lists of sources, organisations and reference material, and, at a certain point, I would recommend readers to buy it, together with their copy of *Sheppard's Bookdealers in the British Isles* and their subscription to *Bookdealer*. Neither of these are simply lists of, respectively, dealers' names and addresses or books wanted, they contain a quantity of other information that you miss at your peril.

The point at which the reader should buy comes, as you would expect me to say, some time after they have read this book. It is relatively slight and it will be updated regularly if the demand justifies it. The first half deals very largely with whether the aspiring bookseller should go into the business in the first place, whether he or she should go full time, how to minimise the risks and why it is so important for everyone in the business to adhere to certain standards.

I devoted much of my time when I was vice-president of the ABA (Antiquarian Booksellers' Association) some years ago to shepherding through a considerable updating of the rules of that body. Among other things, I have also been responsible for putting those rules into the front of the association's annual handbook and on to their new Internet search engine. Except in its esoteric upper reaches, this business is a trade and not a profession, to use two terms that I feel are anyway becoming rather dated now. To most people the word 'antiquarian' signifies little, whereas the word 'secondhand' or, in America, 'used', immediately resonates. Unfortunately, that resonation is not all that positive, although perhaps it is somewhat better when connected with books than with cars or furniture. That is a hurdle we must all get over if we are to run the kind of businesses of which we can be proud and happy. I have a repeated saying that, when one buys books, one "has to live with oneself afterwards". I have tried to live by that tenet for almost forty-five years now.

Richard Joseph, my publisher, has been very patient with me and it may well be that what he is getting is not quite what he originally envisaged. I cannot go into minute detail about bookselling abbreviations and then advise the reader not to use them. I like reference books, but, like many other booksellers who have lots of them, I use only a few. Above all, I think that much of the wisdom accumulated by myself and others over recent decades is being outdated at a frightening rate and I have tried to take this into account. I still know men deeply versed in the ins and outs of Linotype hot-metal typesetting machines, but they don't write books on that expertise any more.

In the second half I have tried to look at where I think the trade and the various technologies now connected with it are likely to go in the near future. This is the section which will be most comprehensively updated with each edition. I would be deluding myself if I pretended to know all the answers even to the situation as it is now. None the less, in my various trade guises I have seen a lot of the inside of the new developments and I hope I can view them with an open mind.

I love reading books, I love the browsing customer and I still own and sell thousands upon thousands of cheap books as well as the occasional fine one. I hope that that love comes through in these pages, but before you pitch yourself and perhaps your family into the undoubted risks of bookdealing, remember that it is a business and subject to the same ground rules as almost any other business.

Paul Minet
April 2000

Part I

Late Twentieth Century

CHAPTER I

General Principles

A HEALTH WARNING

Perhaps I should have had my publisher put a notice on the outside of this book along the lines of a health warning. There will be a fair amount of political incorrectness herein, for it will be a book written for those who wish to sell secondhand books to the general public. Many bookdealers are really happier selling books to each other: after all, one talks the same language, knows the same books, lets drop the same 'in' phrases. There is no need to convince anyone that a book is worth buying for its content, no need for inventiveness and creativity.

Who, then, am I addressing? Perhaps I should start by excluding certain classes of putative bookdealer (and 'bookdealer' is not a word habitually used by the up-market trade – like 'punter', only not so bad). If you want to deal in very expensive antiquarian books, it is probably better, although quite difficult, to think in terms of an apprenticeship with one of the top bookshops or with a specialist dealer. Unless you are a 'natural', of whom more anon, it is probably best to get a good degree, sell yourself to one of the major players, perhaps working for nothing at first, and then find out fairly rapidly whether you have got what it takes. Provided that you have a good memory and the sort of intelligence that would make you go far in almost any business, you may well find yourself before many decades have passed either in a good managerial position or working for yourself as a fine niche antiquarian specialist. By the time you succeed, you may well find yourself on a reasonable mid-manager wage, and your life will be satisfying, if highly risky. If you aspire to that, read this book for recreation, for you may not get much else out of it.

I mentioned the 'natural' bookseller, of whom I have known a number. There is no doubt that there are some aspiring booksellers who seem to know a good book almost by instinct. As often as not, they will have been dabbling in 'running' almost from their schooldays, aided by a very retentive memory which enables them to remember from shop to shop what seems to be in demand. The expression 'running' means just that, moving books from shop to shop in search of better prices. Such natural booksellers should, if they wish to enter the upper reaches of the trade, follow the advice given above. If, on the other hand, they simply wish to make a reasonable living and particularly if they have no capital, they may find some of this book quite useful.

There is another relatively satisfying way to make a mark in this trade. This is to come into books from the specialist end. Someone who has a passion for cars, for instance, may find that collecting actual cars does not suit their means or their lifestyle, so they collect books on cars. After a time almost all book collectors find that they learn enough about their interest to pick up underpriced books which, if they already have them, they can sell on in order to finance their own collecting. From this, it is but a step to small catalogues, book fairs and, in a minority of cases, a full-time career. Picking up the expertise of selling – cataloguing, collation, pricing, etc. – is relatively easy given the expertise in the content to start with. I will deal with various aspects of these matters in due course.

One word of caution should be uttered at this stage: there is a great gulf between living on an outside salary and selling the odd book for profit on the one hand, and selling books for a living on the other. It may seem quite easy, once you have picked up some rudimentary knowledge, to buy a book for, say, four pounds in a boot sale or a general shop and then sell it on at ten pounds to a proper bookseller. It is a very different matter if you *have* to do it many times a week in order to eat. This is a very high risk business, where the accumulation of books under your bed or in your garage is extremely easy, but the turning of them into real cash is extremely difficult. As I remarked in my preface, my last book put off quite a lot of aspiring full-timers and I used to boast of that. Unless you are super-confident, stick to your salary and do your bookselling on the side, pay off the mortgage, get the kids through university and make sure your husband or wife has a well-paid job before embarking on these treacherous waters.

Having got that warning out of the way and also defined to some extent those I am not addressing, let me get down to my actual proposed audience. It would be quite impossible to delineate a typical secondhand bookdealer, for it is the most disparate trade, with people drifting in (and often temporarily out) from all directions. It is in many cases now a second career and there is no doubt that the fifty-five-ish retiree with an early pension behind him does have a certain advantage. There are, of course, some young people, wives (who often end up employing their husbands) and people who, having said all their working lives to bookseller acquaintances like me that "I have always wanted to be a bookseller", do actually take the plunge. There are something like four thousand people vaguely, often very vaguely, connected with the secondhand and rare-book business in Britain, of whom I should be surprised if there are five hundred who actually earn a living at it. So, let us suppose, dear reader, that you ignore the health warning above and

15

decide to become a part-time or full-time bookdealer; where do you go from here?

WHAT ARE YOU TRYING TO DO?

It is not a bad idea to give yourself some kind of medium-term aim. Let us assume that you have attended the odd book fair, know your local bookshop reasonably well and have some actual interest in reading or collecting books. Do you see yourself eventually sitting in a house in the country cataloguing books and spending days hunting for rarities? That is by no means an unusual aim and in fact describes, in rather simplistic terms, what most booksellers in this country actually do. Would you like to find a shop and sell books to a beloved clientele from behind a counter? That is becoming rather a dated concept now, but it is not impossible. It deserves a chapter on its own and it will receive one. You may think of yourself as a permanent part-timer, buying odd books in jumble sales or beating the dealers at their own game and then selling books on by quoting into the trade. That also is a common aspiration and not an unreasonable one, which will be covered in these pages. If you actually plan to see yourself bidding wildly at Sotheby's or Christie's, go back to square one above and learn rare bookselling properly. You may, if you start as a minor specialist, build up to buying and selling fine and expensive books in your subject, perhaps even through the London auctions, but even then you will probably want so few books that you will telephone in your bid rather than attend.

When I was first asked to write this book, I had a certain idea of what I wanted to say. I would, I thought, distil forty years of messing around in books into a smattering of wisdom. I have never made much in books, although I have turned over a great deal of money (as my trade colleagues have been quick to point out), but the reader can learn from my mistakes. In the past year or two, however, I have seen a sea change in bookselling, with the result that what you are about to read differs markedly from what I would have written a year ago. In some ways the picture is more hopeful. I think some of the fun I have had will be harder to come by. It will still be one of the riskier businesses. Above all, I think it is going to be different and I hope to give some idea of how I think it will become different.

FIRST STEPS

It will be clear from the above that, whether you are well heeled or not, you must ease into this business. My mother ran a small book business and I suppose I learnt something from her. I was quoting books on postcards to established dealers before I left school, but my idea, perhaps not an unusual one in those days, was simply to find a shop to let, shelve it as best I could, buy some books and open up. I think I must have opened about six shops over the following years before I became more systematic, although I have never quite broken myself of the habit.

That is not the course I would recommend nowadays. There are certainly empty shops around, but they are expensive in terms of rents, rates and help. In the past forty years the price of secondhand books has not kept pace with inflation and it seems unlikely to catch up now. If you feel you must have a shop, reconcile yourself to the fact that it will be several steps, if not several years, down the road. If you absolutely must, find yourself several partners prepared to put some money in and make sure that one at least of them knows what he or she is doing – and then don't take any money out to live on for quite a long time.

Having disposed of that non-option, let us consider what you should do. The primary answer is that slogan of the present government (I am assuming I can alter my terminology as editions of this book succeed one another), 'education, education, education'. I am sorry if you have accomplished lots of these steps before coming to this book, but I am going to be basic:

(a) visit every venue in your neighbourhood where books are to be had and look at their prices. Remember that the vast majority of books are first editions, never having run to a second. If you are visiting a bookshop and the bookseller has written 'first edition' inside great quantities of his stock, he probably doesn't know what he is doing (unless he is Rota, or Jarndyce, or Bell, Book and Radmell, but then you shouldn't be in their shops at this stage in your learning curve). Boot fairs, jumble sales, junk shops and the smaller bookshops will be your stamping ground at this stage, with the essential addition of book fairs. You can find out more about book fairs from two magazines, *Antiquarian Book Monthly* and *Bookdealer*, and also by getting on the mailing list of the two main trade associations, the Antiquarian Booksellers' Association (ABA) and the Provincial Booksellers' Fairs Association (PBFA).

(b) Do not buy anything much unless you absolutely have to. What you are doing is learning, not stocking up. Obviously, if you are still earning a fat salary in a City bank or something of the sort and you see what is clearly a drastically under-priced book, buy it – but not if you cannot afford to keep it for the next few years. If you are going down the road of specialisation from the beginning, be extra careful. Only buy books in good condition or very good books in tatty condition at giveaway prices (*cf.* notes on binding). Be extra cautious about reference works, which have a weird fascination for all booksellers, many of whom think that having a room full of vaguely literary reference books absolves them from filling their brains with facts. There are some obvious books which, if you can afford it, will always be of use and your reading of other people's catalogues will point you in their direction, but it is your head which you are trying to prime. Everything else comes second.

It is a regrettable fact that most of the dealers in *Sheppard's* work from home, so their stocks are not really available for browsing, although some of them will exhibit in book fairs and you may be able to get to terms with them there. Both trade associations will supply you with lists of their members and these lists include specialities. Many of those listed will send you catalogues upon request (do not mention, obviously, that you need them as textbooks rather than buying lists). If you find them of no interest, it is courteous to ask to be removed from their mailing list in order to stop them wasting money. It is probably not worthwhile at this stage buying the standard works on prices. I would be surprised if any of them last long and in any case the Internet is looming over that whole field (see later).

When looking in bookshops, do not restrict yourself to examining the books and prices which interest you. There are various books that crop up in almost all bookshops and a comparison of their prices will give you some clue as to the competence of the shop owner.

The outstanding work in this field is a very attractive book called *The Scallop*, finely printed and illustrated and found nearly everywhere. Shell, the publishers, once gave away two hundred and fifty thousand copies to their shareholders and any bookseller who prices it above, say, seven pounds fifty does not know his business. You will soon learn to recognise others.

Having followed this regimen for some time, you should be able to form some idea as to what you want to do next. If you wish to buy and sell more or less any book you can turn over at a profit, you can take a subscription to *Bookdealer* and start quoting books requested by the dealers therein (some nineteen thousand per week, it is said). You can use the experience in pricing gained from your previous researches into bookshops and catalogues and the latter will also give you some idea as to how to describe the books. *Always under-describe.* Nobody ever returned a book because it was better than they expected, whereas the opposite is all too common. It is always better to go for a relatively modest profit at this stage rather than quote very high and get only one in fifty quotes. You are looking for goodwill and experience rather than a living and you may well find that, after a certain number of successes, you will be sent wants lists and requests by those to whom you are selling. Most of these remarks, incidentally, apply equally to those who have decided to work through the Internet. Do not rush into a web site which you are unable to sustain with a flow of reasonable books. What you are after just now is credible quoting and a toehold in what is essentially a fairly small and clubbable trade. Barry Shaw, who runs *Bookdealer*, is an old friend of mine. He is vastly sympathetic to small dealers and can be helpful, although he is a busy man. He tumbles to unsatisfactory dealers very quickly. His magazine is extremely efficient and subscribing to it is undoubtedly one of the key steps into the secondhand-book trade.

The other magazine I mentioned, *Antiquarian Book Monthly*, is useful for its book fairs list, its advertisements, reviews of catalogues and auctions and a range of general articles. It tends, nowadays, to neglect what one might call older antiquarian books (pre-1800) but this is a reflection of changing tastes in collecting. If you are a real glutton for punishment, you can read the column I have written in it for the past twenty-five years.

To cast back a little, say you decide that general quoting is not your eventual aim, I would suggest that you do a certain amount of it simply to get your hand in with descriptions and test your eye for a bargain. Other dealers will often tell you you have a bargain, but it is only if someone buys it from you that you know it actually is one. Never forget that the books on the shelves in booksellers' shops and those still around in book fairs when you get in (and you get in two or three hours after the dealers who are exhibiting), are those that have not sold. It may be some time before you can regularly second guess both the dealer and his customers.

Anyway, say you dabble in general quoting but it doesn't really interest you, then your alternative is specialisation, which I would recommend to anyone nowadays whether they intend to deal in general books or not. You can have either a minor specialisation, usually something that interests you personally, or a major specialisation, in which case you are looking at a comprehensive stock built up over a period. I will devote a separate chapter to that second option. Most smaller dealers will combine a general business with a modest specialisation.

You are now getting a little deeper into it. Hopefully, you have not done anything rash like leaving your job, although you may of course have had your job leave you. If that has happened, resist the temptation to sink any redundancy money into a load of books at the local auction, unless the sum of money involved is very small. Mind you, if you feel that such a habit is creeping up on you, you might keep an eye open for a sound secondhand Volvo estate and trade your run-about in for that, but that may be running ahead a little.

Let us stick with the general scene, leaving the real specialities until later. You should by now have got some basics: your *Bookdealer* subscription and the quotation forms that go with it; a few reference books; some catalogues, especially those in your chosen field; some shelving at home; a few trade contacts. You are now fit for building up a small *part-time* business at home and I would advise you to do this for a minimum of a couple of years. Plough the money back – you will probably find yourself putting more in, but keep it under some kind of control, anyone can trade comfortably if they keep on feeding money in and accumulating books (that thought comes from abundant experience). Try to work to some kind of business plan, even if it is only chopping some books out if the garage gets too full.

THE BIG DECISION

Jumping to the end of the two years or whatever time you think appropriate, you will now have cut some of your teeth in this business. If you are to specialise, you may have got together the skeleton of your basic stock. If you wish to become a general dealer, you may also have some non-specialist books, although the like-lihood is that it will be what you have failed to sell by post or Internet. Unless you have been very lucky indeed with your purchasing, you will have made nothing like enough to live on. So stick with whatever you were living off before and face your next decision.

You can at this stage do one of two things: you can continue to quote books, sell through an Internet site and treat your bookselling as a part-time interest. There is nothing wrong in this. Indeed, I suspect that perhaps forty per cent of those in *Sheppard's* come under this heading. It is rewarding in money and interest, you keep your risks to a minimum and you have plenty of time for family and other interests. If you collect books yourself, you can also pick up items for your own collection, usually at trade price.

Your other choice is to move into another phase before you go full time. This will involve working many weekends, a certain amount of investment in books, collapsible bookcases, an estate car and a few other expenses, all affordable and still aimed at keeping your options open. But by moving into the book fair scene as a general bookseller, the likelihood is that you will meet a lot of nice people (booksellers, in my experience, are usually nice people) and potential customers and, gradually, you will want to go further into this fascinating business. You stand, therefore, at some kind of crossroads.

CHAPTER II

Part Time through to Full Time

NOT SO FULL TIME

The crossroads mentioned at the end of the last chapter is not whether to stay in bookselling – I am assuming you took that decision some time back. It is the crucial decision whether to embark on the business full time. A very large proportion of those dealing in books work virtually full time at it but actually pay much of their living costs in a variety of ways, with bookselling contributing only part of the total. Some of those earning their living in books resent this method, since it enables its practitioners to take somewhat greater risks or smaller profit margins. I take a fairly relaxed view, suspecting that the total size of the market is increased by such dealers and that, in the end, a larger demand produces somewhat higher prices. There is no doubt that a pension, a working husband or wife (working at something else) or the odd flat let above the shop make things considerably easier. I would also repeat that a careful assessment of your future family living costs can avoid future hardships.

For much of my time in the trade, there was an element of 'moving on' about much retail bookselling. The value of freeholds and leases was rising with inflation and many booksellers would last a few years at one place then sell their property and often their stock, pay their accumulated debts and set up somewhere else. The decline of inflation has made this cycle a lot less common. General stocks are not particularly valuable nowadays, leases are usually very short and the flow of people wishing to enter the retail shop trade is not what it was. It is better to be realistic at the start nowadays, even to the extent of taking into account the difficulty of moving back into the job market as one gets older, i.e. if the experiment doesn't work.

I am sorry if the last two paragraphs read pessimistically. If I can impress upon the reader the risks involved in secondhand dealing as well as its pleasures, I will not be unhappy.

Let us now assume that you wish to press on into full-time bookselling. There are two options, as mentioned above. The commoner one is to convert part of your home into a bookroom or storage. One of your aims is to avoid wages, so take full advantage of modest electronics by installing an answerphone, a fax and probably now e-mail. This will free you to split your time into three – time to get out looking for stock; weekends for book fairs; and an inevitable period for dealing with orders, cataloguing, quoting, collating purchases, cleaning stock, reading other people's lists, studying *Bookdealer* and all those tasks which cut into the essential business of finding saleable stock.

Many home booksellers find the effort of attending or exhibiting at book fairs too great, but I would definitely recommend one or the other, preferably both. It is very important to keep an eye on demand, prices and what other traders are doing. If you are aiming for a narrow specialisation, it is probable that simple attendance at all your local book fairs will be enough, in addition to habitual combing of every other source of stock you can find. On balance, I think specialisation requires a chapter to itself, so I will cease for the moment to discuss that option except in so far as all general dealers should have something in which they can excel.

For the more general home dealer, at least in their early years, actual exhibiting at fairs will have solid advantages. Some parts of the country are better than others for the novice, who will have to find fairs unconnected with the two major bookselling organisations, the ABA and the PBFA. For these smaller fairs, all that is required is pre-booking, a small sum of money for the stand and some stock to put out. Apart from a certain flow of takings, the main advantages consist of being able to view and buy books in the hour or two before the fair opens, and in getting to know other local dealers in an atmosphere of shared endeavour. This is where your old estate car, your folding bookshelves and an ability to get up fairly early will all come in handy. On a very basic level, I am always astonished by the flimsy trolleys many book-sellers use to transport their books into and out of fairs: to avoid spending a paltry fifty pounds, they suffer years of inconvenience. What are called agricultural dump trolleys are the best and stoutest option.

I may also have skated over a consideration which can be crucial. If your conscience is against working on Sunday, you are blocking off a major part of the book fair scene. It is also advisable to think very carefully about the family implications of doing a lot of weekend book fairs (and they are almost all then). If your wife/husband is working full time elsewhere, your time together is going to shrink drastically and your prime time with your children, if they are still young, will also diminish.

TRADE ORGANISATIONS

Once you have been dealing for a couple of years and have acquired some friends to back your application, you should join the PBFA, which will offer you a number of advantages. The main one is that you can exhibit at a range of fairs in London and around the country, fairs of a better quality, on the whole, than the small ones organised by smaller organisations. There is one exception to this judgement, a company called The Exhibition Team or perhaps HD Bookfairs (which are the same), of which more anon. As well as providing you with the opportunity to exhibit at their book fairs, the PBFA will provide you with a useful Newsletter, with the opportunity to buy various supplies jointly (notably folding bookshelves, notice boards and bags), and with a branch structure which will be both sociable and commercially useful. My personal feeling is that, as an organisation, it is currently (early 2000) slightly in need of reinventing itself, but for the aspiring bookdealer, membership is essential. I was one of the original six members and the way its organisation has refined itself has been fascinating.

The senior trade organisation, the ABA, is a different kettle of fish, but, since entry is quite difficult and you need a five years' trade record to get in, we had better postpone comment on that until later.

In the early stages, it is probably better to confine oneself to provincial book fairs, avoiding London. The Russell Fair, which is the major PBFA monthly fair in Bloomsbury, is valuable for selling to the informed public, but this presupposes a good stock to offer. Many of those who do exhibit there seem to me not to rotate their stock enough, which imparts a certain sameness to their stands from month to month. For trade buying, the smaller fairs are better and, in the early stages, the novice is into very selective buying indeed. If you must exhibit in London, the better bet is the rather larger, disparate fairs run in the Royal National on the second Sunday of the month by The Exhibition Team. The Fairs are extremely hard work and, if you are to search them properly, an assistant or perhaps a husband or wife to run your own stand is almost essential. The stock offered is wide and bargains are very possible. Later in the day, or when that fair has closed, it can be useful to visit the Russell nearby, which closes later. Very recently, the PBFA have started a second fair at the Post House in the same area, open on Sunday only rather than on Sunday and Monday. Allowing for some time on your own stand, it is almost impossible to cover every stand of all three fairs in the time available but a few visits should enable you to spot which stands to skip.

Wherever you exhibit, turn up early and organise your boxes and bookcases properly so that you have time to look at everyone else's stand before the public gets in. It is almost impossible to cover even the Royal National in detail before it opens, so it becomes important to note which stands you find most interesting from month to month and concentrate on those, leaving the others until later. With the smaller provincial fairs, it should be possible to cover the whole fair before opening time. Some of the better ones even offer rather good food for exhibitors and customers alike. The best list is probably that in *Antiquarian Book Monthly*, although sometimes it is useful to look also in the small-ads column in the back of *Bookdealer*. Once you are a PBFA member, you will be sent a comprehensive list of all their fairs months in advance. I understand that ABM is making arrangements for one of the new web sites, Biblion, to carry their book fairs listings.

A word about terms. It is customary to offer ten per cent discount to the trade and, as you get better known, this will become automatic. Obviously, it is possible to make offers, but it is only really acceptable to do this late in the day. To offer a sharp reduction even before the fair opens seems to me unreasonable. Dealers can put books aside under the stand for purchase later in the day, but *you must* put a trade card in it. It is not acceptable to reserve a book and haggle later: if you reserve it, you must pay the marked price less ten per cent unless a prior agreement has been made. It is customary to pay on the day at fairs, although some major dealers ask for bills to be sent. My feeling is that this is only reasonable for substantial purchases. The smaller the fair and the smaller the dealer, the more you should strive to pay up before the end of the day and not quibble too much about the price. There is a slightly different approach applicable to bookshops, which I will detail later.

OUTSIDE THE BOOK FAIR

Moving on from fairs, the beginner should continue to research all other local sources for profitable purchases. On the whole, buying books singly is expensive, especially where cheap books are concerned. This does not matter where the book concerned is expensive. For instance, to travel some distance, take a risk on one book, collate it, perhaps clean it and incur the costs of passing it on, whether by catalogue or by direct quote, all for a gross profit of less than (say) ten pounds is hardly worthwhile. Yet, with the real specialist, this will be a common experience. If you travel around searching, it is better to cast your net wider, aim to buy a certain number of books for a total of a hundred pounds or more, spread the risk and the costs of your time. This is, of course, the attraction of the book fair, where supplies are concentrated. At the same time, however, the stock at book fairs is combed more thoroughly by your competitors. Even with the small dealer, you may be looking, almost by definition, for the book he does *not* think worth taking to a fair, but which you know someone who wants. Small retail shops are, unfortunately, getting scarcer, for reasons dealt with in these pages, as are the junkier type of 'antique' shop and the general secondhand shop. Boot sales require hard work and getting there very early, although jumble sales, at least in country areas, remain fruitful. Very valuable books offered at boot sales should be viewed with some suspicion as possibly stolen, although certain areas of Britain are taking steps to tighten up on them. Charity shops are becoming too knowledgeable and many of the better books now contributed to them are syphoned off to larger branches or even to London auctions. At a modest level, however, the charity shop has in many ways taken over from the smaller local bookshop (minus the expertise).

I do not propose to say a great deal about auctions. Almost every country area has its ration of auctions and its nucleus of dealers who frequent or at least view every sale. Large general lots are often worth buying, although it is as well to check that what you viewed is still what is being offered. Moving books from lot to lot in small auctions is common. When you become known, you may be approached by other dealers to form 'rings', which are not only illegal and dishonest but are also firmly barred to members of trade organisations. In my experience, a very firm refusal on the part of the fledgling dealer at an early stage will lead to an acceptance that he has strong feelings on the subject. Bar an occasional rogue bid, he will then be left alone. There are in any case so many semi-professionals and discriminating amateurs bidding at auctions these days that the scandals of the past, when owners were effectively swindled out of their libraries, are becoming largely historic.

The rules about buying books in auctions are basically the same as buying anything else this way. Remember that, at least in smaller auctions, books are normally sold 'as seen', i.e. not subject to return, so they must be properly viewed. Set yourself a price and do not exceed it, or at least not by much. I could name a number of dealers who have been ruined by an inability to stop bidding. Be prepared to spend time viewing and time attending and walk away with nothing. If you are not prepared to do this, don't go! When I have done well at auction, it is almost always by buying a large lot which deters the casual buyer by its size.

As well as the general auction, there are now a number of auctioneers outside London who 'specialise' in books. The best is probably Y Gelli in Hay-on-Wye, who take some trouble over their lots, although even there one must remember that a fair number of the lots will be put in by other dealers. Other provincial auctioneers now have an obnoxious habit of cataloguing the books individually or in small lots, as if they were London auctioneers, and then refusing to take responsibility for faults. This is unfair, since anyone pretending to be a specialist should accept the responsibilities that go with the higher prices achieved (that maxim applies to specialist booksellers as well as specialist auctioneers). As I write, efforts are being made by the trade organisations to regularise this situation.

THE GRIND OF PAPERWORK

One of the advantages of running a retail bookshop is that it keeps the paperwork to a minimum. Working from home, conversely and perhaps perversely, leads to a great deal of paperwork. Almost all e-mails lead to a number of exchanges before a satisfactory deal is concluded, catalogues generate paperwork whether the customer gets the book ordered or not, quotations of books wanted lead to books being put aside for various periods and payments can get out of control far too easily. Some of my tips on these subjects will be scattered through pages further on, but it is simply not possible to reduce paperwork below a certain level. As a self-employed person, you will need to retain a certain level of records for the tax and VAT man and it is probably better to keep too much rather than too little. The theory is that the computer is ushering in a paperless society but that is not my experience. At the very least, back everything up on disc. There are also quite large areas of the book business which still lend themselves to physical records. It is worth registering for VAT at an early stage, since bookselling is one of the few trades that are zero-rated, i.e. you get your VAT spending back without having to charge any. It is usually worthwhile to register even before you reach the turnover level at which it becomes obligatory.

If you issue catalogues, always produce a master copy and write down in it every order you receive for items in it. There are, of course, items which you will never see again, but the bulk of my wants list comes from duplicate orders and quotes based on these are highly successful, sometimes years later.

There are still many booksellers who invoice books ordered from catalogues by their customers, at least anyone they have dealt with before. I used to do this and, like others, I very rarely had real unpaid bills. What I did have, however, was the bother of sending statements and chasing late payers. It is still the custom to invoice other traders, although it is not a bad idea to check their bona fides at least as far as seeing if they are in the standard trade lists. Institutions, libraries and such, will also expect to be invoiced and their orders should be on headed notepaper. Nowadays, I offer credit to no one else, since ninety-nine per cent of people have credit cards. Let the credit-card companies take the strain. For those who have not, we will put the book aside for a stated period so that they can send a cheque. My assistants and I have done this for so long that we ask for cards or make arrangements without embarrassment and customers accept this. Not only does this cut paperwork, it improves the speed of cash turnround no end. We run quite a large outfit here and I am very rarely owed in excess of a thousand at any one time.

There are various small matters to remember under the heading of paperwork. It pays to get something respectable done in the way of a trade card. Other dealers, at book fairs and elsewhere, are impressed and personal customers equally so, whether they are thinking of selling books to you or if they simply wish to have a record of you for future use. Invoices should be numbered, not necessarily by machine but just to keep them in order. Always make sure, above all, that books sold are noted as sold, especially by telephone. Explaining to a dedicated collector why the book you promised him was in fact sold before he phoned and had not been noted is one of the worst experiences in this business.

KEEPING TRACK OF STOCK

Sticking with the home dealer, some initial thought should be given to where to keep your books. Whether you are investing in proper bookcases spread around your house or installing planks resting on bricks in an outhouse or garage, the vital prerequisite is that the storage place be dry. For books in use, I usually prefer to keep away from glass-fronted bookcases, which are awkward and not always as dry as one would think. When viewing books in a customer's house with a view to purchase, always take them out and examine them carefully. They may well have been there a long time and their overall condition may not match up to their spines. For stock storage, a system of numbering shelves and matching catalogue entries to shelf numbers saves lots of time and is probably better than rigid classification. If you put, say, all your theatre books in one bookcase and then buy another large lot, the rearrangement involved becomes complicated. The person who needs to find these books is yourself, whereas in a bookshop the customer's convenience comes first.

If you are doing regular book fairs, give some thought to revolving your stock, which does not mean moving everything up to the attic and back each month. I know booksellers who keep twenty boxes of books in their garage, simply loading them back into the car each time with replacements for books sold last time. That is not the way to build fresh custom. It is hard work to change books around, but it pays off in the end.

As regards what you should take to a fair, complications can arise. Say you are a general bookseller with a sideline in country books. What you really want to do is to sell general books to the other dealers at the fair, with perhaps a few to the public also, but to buy country books as well as bargains from the other stands. If you take a selection of your good country books, the other dealers will see what you charge for them, whereas you want to buy from them cheaply. Most fairs, in my view, fulfil two functions: they enable you to buy well and they provide a way of capitalising on what you don't want. One hopes to come away with a surplus of cash over purchases, but that in a way is a bonus.

This view of book fairs assumes that what you really want is to consolidate yourself in the trade. Book-fairs were in their heyday in Britain in the 1980s. I went into their origins in some detail in my book *Late Booking* and there is no doubt that, in their early days, they performed a very valuable function in bringing book-sellers, books and customers together at a time when retail bookshops were in steep decline. It is now my view, that, although they will survive, there will be fewer of them in years to come. I think the impact of the Internet will lessen their usefulness and that there may even be a modest revival in retail shops bolstered by Internet sales. The coming dealer should use them now but should aim to diversify into other fields in due course. This will involve building some kind of specialisation as well as listing general books in catalogues and on the Internet. While fairs survive, they should be used for building stock and recruiting customers, but the dealer looking a few years ahead might well think in wider terms.

THE TWO ASSOCIATIONS

At this stage I should, perhaps, say a few words about the two trade associations. Membership of one or the other or both is, in my view, essential to anyone seriously proposing to build a first or second career in bookdealing. As I have noted, I was one of the six original members of the Provincial Booksellers' Fairs Association and I have for many years been a member of the Antiquarian Booksellers' Association, recently as its president. It is my view, which has been disputed in the past, that the two bodies perform different functions and that they are not candidates for amalgamation. This is quite awkward, since the ABA is a member of the International League of Antiquarian Booksellers, while the PBFA is not. This means that only the former's members may partici-pate in major international fairs. To my knowledge, there is no other country with two such respectable associations and the rule about one ILAB associate per country is unlikely to be changed. This has most recently come to the fore over the foundation of an ABA/ILAB search engine on the Internet, which excludes PBFA members who are not also in the ABA. There is, however, a liaison committee bridging the two and some seventy-five per cent of ABA members are in the PBFA so the problems should not be exaggerated. Unfortunately, proposals to run joint book fairs, which have occasionally seemed very sensible in particular situations, have sometimes foundered on the fact that there are in the PBFA some members who have been denied entry into the older association for one reason or another (although the reasons are never given by either association).

It would be invidious to go into much detail as to why I consider the two associations fulfil separate roles. One obvious difference is that members of the ABA have to be full time, whereas those of the PBFA do not. Hence my advice to go for membership of the younger and larger association first and only subsequently, when your path has been set, you have taken the plunge into full-time bookselling and you feel you may need the somewhat wider national and international services offered by the ABA, apply to join them. Most ABA members manage to combine membership of both without any clash of interest. There have been signs in recent years that the PBFA has been moving closer to the fairly rigid code of practice enforced by the ABA and this is to be welcomed. This is a trade dependent upon a public perception that it is trustworthy and this must be the fundamental aim of both associations to foster and maintain.

CHAPTER III

Retail If You Must

DEVELOPING FURTHER

I am now going to abandon the chronological approach assumed so far. The options before the career or part-career bookdealer have now opened out too far to justify this approach. Speaking in current terms, our bookdealer should now be turning over a minimum of around fifty thousand per annum, divided between book fairs, direct quoting and sales through lists or the Internet. He or she may also be putting the occasional lot into auction locally and, if they are lucky, selling the occasional 'find' to the London trade or through the London auctions. By now they will almost certainly have taken the plunge into the June Book-fair season, probably through either the PBFA or the Exhibition Team fairs held in the first half of that month and they may also have achieved stands at the PBFA York or Oxford fairs. If they are successful and have some modest capital behind them, they could well be putting out some kind of specialist catalogue and be tempted to bolster their specialist stock with the odd purchase at the London auctions.

If they move to these higher levels, I think their turnover should be significantly above that fifty thousand pound minimum. The more ambitious the stock handled, the lower will be the margin. Obviously, a fifty-thousand pound turnover will need, roughly speaking, a gross profit margin in excess of fifty per cent to justify the bookseller calling himself full time. With low-priced books and lots of hard work, a gross margin of sixty per cent should be achievable, but clearly a dealer handling more expensive stock and turning over, say, a hundred and fifty thousand pounds will be working on slimmer margins, with greater risks and (unless he is very lucky) utilising more capital in the shape of overdrafts or loans. It is here that the advantage of the dealer with a pension or other source of income is demonstrated. A partial income of ten thousand pounds removed from a business and bolstered in other ways is a very different matter from one of twenty-five thousand pounds or more which would still be only slightly above the current average wage. Yet to remove twenty-five thousand pounds from a business which is still investing into more and better stock, or building a specialist stock, may well prove a strain.

Let us therefore leave the potential specialist or the part-timer who does not yet quite dare to become full time to their own devices and take a look at the shop option.

For the past twenty years shops have been very much the tough option in this business. City centres are notoriously expensive and one would now be extremely lucky to find a halfway decent shop anywhere near a city centre at under fifteen thousand pounds per annum. If it is much lower, it probably needs significant money spent on it or it is well off the beaten track. Anyone owning a modest shop at present will, if they have any sense, be seeking to convert it into living accommodation, which is worth much more than minor shop property. Councils are becoming more sympathetic to such conversions now and this is, in my opinion, to the good, since it will take a deal of grade two and three shop property into residential use instead of charity shops or under-capitalised ventures that will never succeed. (Yes, this may well include you, but...)

The halfway decent shop mentioned above probably has another five thousand pounds or so property rates on top of its rent, plus the usual costs of lighting, heating, insurance, etc. But these deterrents pale into insignificance beside the question of staff. Do not run away with the idea that it is possible to install some semi-charitable old lady to run the shop while you are away. Customers nowadays expect some kind of informed assistance. Above all, your shop must be open when you say it will be open. Unexpected closing is one of the banes of the book trade and nothing puts the average collector or dealer off more than to travel miles on the off chance you may have something good, and then find you shut. You will have to pay some kind of assistant a reasonable wage (even the statutory minimum wage adds up and you probably won't get away with that in a town centre). In addition, they must be reliable, able to cope with at least basic questions about the stock and be absolutely honest. It is almost impossible to keep a check on sales money in a secondhand bookshop, since the type of stock does not lend itself to accurate stocktaking: you rely on the assistant's honesty. I think it is almost impossible to run a respectable shop with basic overheads of under forty thousand pounds these days, *plus* whatever you need to take out to live on. If your stock is costing you fifty per cent, therefore, your breakeven point is going to be around the hundred-thousand-pound mark unless you own the property yourself.

It may be that you have a husband, wife or child who can be left in charge, in which case you have a head start, but they must be reasonably knowledgeable or at the very least extremely reliable and sensible.

Why have staff at all? Why not just spend your time behind the counter cleaning and collating books, exchanging literary gossip with customers and drinking coffee? We had, I think, better have a rule here. If you want to build a proper shop rather than simply a base for operations, do not spend more than three days a week in that shop. During those three days, do your paperwork, clean and collate your books, make appointments for your good customers to visit you, catalogue your books for the Internet, order books through *Bookdealer* and do all the hundred and one other things you need do in the shop. Then spend the other three of your working days (you didn't think there were only five working days in the week, did you?) elsewhere, viewing customers' books, visiting other bookshops, doing jumble sales, going to book fairs, getting the feel of other people's market in books so that you can translate it back to your own shop.

In other bookshops, don't just look at books you might buy: look at copies of books you already have and see what the other dealer is charging for them. Try to understand why books are priced as they are, if only to disagree with them. On this question you have a tool available to you that is, at least at present, bidding fair to be invaluable, the priced offerings on the Internet. Until recently we could look a good book up in *Book Auction Records* (BAR), but that was always a little hit or miss. It had to be a good book above a certain value; you had to recognise that it was such, but worse still there was no way of creating prices. As I write, BAR has been acquired by an Internet auctioneers called iCollector and seems likely to be available soon free on-line. Back numbers can be found in book fairs and are worth acquiring. In addition, Michael Coles in York has issued a CD-Rom containing some two hundred and fifty thousand assorted catalogue entries which appeared in a series of reference books he issued in the 1990s. This CD is quite useful since it covers an area somewhat lower down the market than BAR and it is not unreasonably priced.

Find out, therefore, what prices other dealers are asking for the books you acquire, then assess them again in the light of those prices and price accordingly. If the book you reckon is an interesting one is not anywhere you look, you have one of two explanations: either your judgement is wrong and the book is common, or it is very uncommon and you can create your own price.

THE SOFTER OPTION

In the past decade or so I have known many people try to start retail shops in or near town centres. Very few of them have lasted the four years I reckon it takes the average shop to get known. Leases are short these days, the landlords brutal and the secondary shop situation is a poor one in most urban situations. (NB There is a current trend for chains of shops to close down in town centres and this may improve the situation for smaller businesses.)

If you must go for a retail shop, look for a small town, a village or even a disused garage showroom some-where on a dual carriageway. Your rent will be lower, or you may be able to buy freehold; your labour will be cheaper and more reliable; even your other overheads may be marginally lower. Furthermore, your trade customers will be able to park, you will be able to load up for book fairs more easily and you may even find, if your position is visible to passing traffic, that you get some reasonable passing trade. Before you accumulate such passing trade, you may well have to wait some time, perhaps the four years mentioned above. In the meantime you can do your book fairs, get out looking for books and for knowledge, build up an Internet business. If in the first two years you manage to get that ten thousand pounds per annum out of the takings without crippling the business, you will be lucky. If you have heavy family commitments and no wife or husband pulling in a steady wage from somewhere else, then the odds are against you, but they are not insuperable. Hard work, a good memory and a modicum of luck, perhaps a good book lot or two, might make all the difference.

I have to say, however, that the retail route will always be the harder of the two. All book businesses, unless they are ruthlessly specialised and well funded, must rest on three or more legs these days. One used to say it could be retail, book fair and catalogue. That may well be retail, book fair and Internet now, with perhaps a bit of running thrown in when times are hard. Later, it might be a combination of some books in some such retail outlet as Biblion in London, plus some carefully selected book fairs, the Internet and a specialised subject. Biblion is a venture in Mayfair which rents serviced bookcases to booksellers in a central and quite luxurious milieu. However specialised you become, do not give up turning up at book fairs, at the very least just to see and hear what is happening in the business. That will almost certainly mean working on some Saturdays and Sundays, since almost all the worthwhile fairs take place at weekends.

Perhaps I should also cover the definition of a shop. It should have a window and the contents of that window should be dusted and changed regularly. The books in the shop itself should also be dusted and moved about. I have, through the years, come across lots of bookshops covered in dust, the books stacked two or three rows deep and the fiction section threatening to take over the place. I have been the one who has cleared them out after they have gone bust, a dusty occupation. In this day and age, regrettable though it may be, the average customer expects to view secondhand books without having to wash his hands immediately afterwards. Said customer would like enough light to read the titles, enough space to stand back a little, if that is the way his eyesight works, and books with spines on them classified in broad general sections.

This matter of classification is an interesting one. There is a well-known bookshop in Essex where everything is divided into minute sections, all beautifully labelled and ruthlessly categorised. I would like to say they do very badly, but they in fact do rather well. I have an assistant at present who is a great believer in strict alphabetical order. I view things slightly differently. I work from the premise that it is extremely unlikely that we will have the exact book a customer wants. The aim is to get him into that book's subject section, since we know that it is a subject that interests him, and then let him look at everything else there, in the hope that he will find something he does not know he wants. If he wants a Muggeridge book, let us say, we do not really want him to go direct to the 'Mug' section of Biography, draw a blank and walk out. Much better he find a biography section where the M's are all vaguely together and he has to do a little work. He may still walk out without his Muggeridge, but he may find something else. I think that the search sections of the Internet will suit the narrowly focused customer well; it is the unfocused – Renaissance-man kind of customer that booksellers like.

DUST WRAPPERS

This brings me to a really contentious area, the dust wrapper or dust jacket as it is perhaps more commonly known these days. I have nothing against dust wrappers. I even try to be patient with the super-finicky first-edition collector whose mania has, in the past few years, become the dust wrapper. I would never purposely pass up the chance of selling anything into the first-editions market in the tattiest wrapper if I could get more money for it that way, while as for cutting the price off a collectable first, I would as soon slit the pages of a Jane Austen first in order to read it.

Where I do depart from the current norm is in my attitude to general secondhand books in poor dust wrappers. The average customer is put off by, let us say, a fifth-edition Batsford topographical book in a dust wrapper with half the spine gone and a large coffee stain on the front, although underneath is a perfectly good hardbacked book. If the wrapper is repairable, repair it. If you must, put it in one of those glossy protective coverings which hide a multitude of sins and often display large areas of white where the title should be found. If, on the other hand, the actual hard cover is in very good condition, you will sell the book faster, display it better and keep your shop tidier if you dispose of the offensive covering. General secondhand bookselling is about selling books for people to read or refer to, not about deterring customers with bits and pieces of wrapper hanging off books and making the shelf look quite different from anything they would have in their own home.

A casual tip – always take credit cards if offered. This is a luxury business in one sense and many booklovers spend more than they can really afford, at least more than they actually have on them. If you put a book aside for someone, and small retailers often do, always put a note on it, something like *we will hold it until the 15th only*, and then put it back on the shelf. The stock is meant to be for sale, not reserved at the back. If you do produce catalogues, I see no particular reason these days for giving credit. The vast majority of people have credit cards and the others can send cheques. The main thing here is to make sure that you or your staff have the patter worked out beforehand 'Right, we still have that. How would you like to pay? We take Visa, Mastercard or Amex, or we could hold it until we receive your cheque.' Say it all naturally – and say it first. If they ask you to send it with an invoice, say that *we* ceased doing that some time ago when credit cards became common. Most booksellers do in fact recover almost all of the payments for the credit they give, but it often takes a deal of hard work. You have other things to do. I have known plenty of booksellers sweat blood over their overdrafts, when they are actually lending the money to their customers interest free! The credit card companies have replaced the tradesman's bill: they are now the experts.

If you do not know what the word 'collate' means, go away and look it up now. All books above twenty pounds should be collated fully. Everything under that can be flipped through in case there are obvious faults, the plates should be checked against the list of illustrations and the binding checked to see if it is loose or the endpapers cracked. The really cheap book can simply be riffled through, especially if it is modern enough to have the plates stitched in rather than tipped in. Close-grained cloth should be cleaned, perhaps with something like Backus Book Restorer (see *Sheppard's*), which also works well on coated dust wrappers. As far as you can, get all your stock on the shelves clean. Leather bindings should be treated with some kind of leather polish, sometimes available in riding shops. I have lost count of the number of mouldy leather books I have seen in book fairs which, given a rub over with some Backus followed by a polish with some good leather polish, would fetch twice the money.

It is incumbent upon booksellers not to deceive customers about the state of a book, but too many of us seem to deceive ourselves, to our own cost. It is the custom in the trade that, should a customer return a book as incomplete, the price is refunded. Even if you suspect sharp practice, it is probably better, at least in most circumstances, simply to pay up. The book must not be put back on the shelf without a proper note of its defect being pencilled in. The initials w.a.f. mean 'with all faults', a reservation which has its uses but which should be used with caution. When you have written it into a book, always point it out to the customer when they buy the book.

To summarise. If you have a bookshop open to the public, make sure you observe the following rules:

- Be open as advertised
- Keep your books clean and tidy
- Keep the money side simple, allowing people to pay as they will
- Keep credit and reservations to the minimum
- Strike a balance between a lease that will lock you in and one that will give you time to develop (better still: own your own freehold)
- Never spend too much time in your own shop.

Nothing mentioned in this book is an exclusive option. I hope I have made it clear that, at least in the early stages, it is a very exceptional bookseller who can earn a living from one of the options available. The novice retailer must get out at weekends to participate in book fairs. The general bookseller can and should have a specialisation. The specialist must utilise every means to acquire his limited selection of customers by combing fairs with catalogues, e-mailed lists and Internet listings.

CHAPTER IV

Acquiring Stock

Faced with empty shelves in a shop or with the spare room fitted up with jumble-sale shelving or shelves supported on bricks, the new bookseller may well feel that he or she will never succeed in filling these vast spaces. The opposite is the truth: 'Books', to coin an old bookselling adage, 'breed'. Unless you are extremely rigorous and specialist, you are bound to end up with lots of books, many of them unsaleable old friends. If you slide in via collecting and part-time dealing, you will go through a number of stages: the straight collection will merge into a collection interlarded with stock; you may then add books you are piling up for a future catalogue; then there are the remains of large auction lots; then the residue from book fairs. It all adds up and before long you will be thinking in terms of putting lots into auction yourself, or calling in a large retailer to buy in bulk (this is almost never a good idea, since it will yield very little).

Do not be afraid of buying reasonably large quantities of books if they are offered, they may well produce new specialities, or stock a shop should you decide to have one, or at the very least enable you to revolve your displays in book fairs. It is not difficult to pile up stock (or mistakes, as some cynics call it), although it must obviously be kept under some sort of control. Be at any rate rigorous about condition. If the book is in poor condition, get it re-bound, sell it off cheap or throw it away. My mother used to say, wisely or not, that there was a customer for every book, but even she, optimist that she was, felt that the book had to be in reasonable condition.

BUYING PRIVATELY

Most booksellers find buying books privately an idea attractive in theory but often awkward and unproductive in practice. The classified advertisement in the local paper, the permanent advertisement in Yellow Pages, the procession through the shop door if you have one, these will all produce the usual crop of people with books which 'must be old because my granny bought it' or people who know it looks tatty but it is always worth offering, for 'you never know what might be valuable'. I have endured and even used the stock phrases for years; it all has to be gone through.

The retail shop draws in its own band of potential sellers. Bear in mind that some people selling the small bundle of rather sad books may be genuinely down to rock bottom for the weekend. Others will bring in several boxes because they are moving, or, will ask you to come out to look at batches of books left them by their parents, lots which always seem to be strong in *Harmsworth Encyclopedias*, copies of *Enquire Within* and incomplete sets of Dickens. It is extraordinarily difficult to get people to specify what they have got, even when they get round to listing them. In any case, our business is in some ways to recognise the value of what they fail to recognise. It all has to be endured, at least in the early stages. Incidentally, one reason for keeping your bookshop tidy and your books in good condition is to demonstrate to customers what you do want to buy. If you exhibit apparent tat, they will try to sell you real tat. It takes time before the real books start to come in and in the meantime you may well find yourself buying quite a lot of books simply to get away, or to say thank you for a cup of tea, or simply because you are sorry for people. Never refuse a cup of tea or coffee. I am a great believer in bonding, or, to put it another way, in the primitive idea about breaking bread with someone being important. I am not suggesting you buy everything, but a reasonably liberal policy will build you a reputation in an area and it is a reputation for fair dealing that will get you the good recommendations in the end.

There is a fair amount of embarrassment in all this. I hope that the day of the real book hustler is now gone. He who would *always* talk everything down, get everything for the lowest possible price and whose offer had more to do with the developing situation than the value of what he was buying. Anyone who says to me that I am the expert and they trust me will get almost too fair a deal from me, certainly more than I might give a fellow dealer. To use that phrase again, you have to live with yourself afterwards. There is, I think, something of an art in what we call the house call. Some people will be hostile and try to hustle you, clearly thinking all dealers are rogues; the only way to deal with this is with firmness and a readiness to walk away with nothing. Most people, however, are extremely pleasant and will take what you say about their books as an honest opinion, as it should be. Through the years, I have had tea with many lonely people who use their books simply to acquire an hour of your time, of anybody's time. I always come away from such calls, which are often rather unproductive, in a suitably chastened frame of mind.

THE HOUSE CALL

One or two tips about house calls. Always tell someone exactly where you are going and leave a slip with the address in your car, just in case. You should remember that a phone call will bring a bookseller to a house and there are oddballs about. I suppose one must say that such precautions apply more particularly to women going into this business, but I have had three rather odd experiences through the years, including one with a person who was undoubtedly mad.

There are fewer large collections of books in private houses than there were. Very occasionally, you will get into a house where there is an old-fashioned family library intact, probably bound in leather and worthy of a real effort. Do not be afraid of making reams of notes and seeking information before a second appointment. Owners of such collections usually know that there is real money involved and will think the better of you for doing it properly. Do not push for a decision; there are often executors or trustees involved, or, at the least, other members of the family, so things will take time. Be civil, correct in your behaviour and fair in your offer. As with auctions, you must be prepared to be outbid in the end. If the offer has been a fair one, it is no disgrace if someone offers more or if they decide to go to auction. If, on the other hand, you have tried to recoup a series of bad buys with one drastic underbid, you will usually lose both the books and your peace of mind nowadays. If you estimate the lot as being beyond your means, approach another big dealer, preferably someone you know you can trust and who is backed by a trade association, and ask for help. A cut and some residual books is better than losing the collection altogether. You will also have done both the seller and the larger dealer a good turn, which may pay off later.

The majority of larger lots, however, do not fall into this category. You may be faced with three or four hundred books, the usual mixture of good and bad, fine and poor condition. If you offer, say, five hundred pounds for such a batch, it may seem to the customer a poor offer, although in fact it may be perfectly fair. What I do is to go carefully through the books sorting them into two piles. One pile, let us say, will consist of about a hundred books, all the good editions and fine copies, while the balance goes into a much larger pile. Offer four hundred pounds for the small pile and a hundred pounds for the larger pile, saying that you do not care whether you get the larger pile or not, but you will only take it if they accept the larger offer for the smaller pile. This indicates the exact position to the seller, i.e. that they have some good books but a lot of indifferent books as well. You will either get the small pile alone (which is, after all, what you really want) or the whole lot at what you originally thought of giving, five hundred pounds. The seller will feel good and you may make some good profit from the larger pile, but at the cost of much hard work.

Variants of this approach can be adopted for smaller lots. This is not to recommend sharp practice: it is a way of getting across, in a crystal-clear manner, just how you are valuing the customer's books. It may even be that it is worth making a separate offer for one or two really good books, but this can be dangerous, as the customer might decide to keep those specific books out and take them to a London auctioneer. If they do say they will do that, make the offer a standing one for a month and the book will often come back. The London auctioneers are now pretty picky about what individual books they accept from private sellers at the lower end of the market, say under three hundred pounds. You can also, of course, warn the customer about the auctioneers' significant charges and long time delays. Don't, however, overdo the negative, which can begin to look a little desperate if you are not careful. It is quite wise to keep away from certain phrases, as well. To look at someone's treasure and say, "Oh, that's terribly common!" can be a great put-down. We know that we mean that there are lots of copies about, but the word 'common' does have other meanings. If you are not going to buy the books or not going to offer much, the seller must be let down lightly. When someone else mentions to them that they are getting rid of books, you want them to say, "Go to [you]. They seem to know what they are doing."

SOLICITORS AND VALUERS

Foster relationships with house-clearers and general dealers, although many of these have to be treated fairly carefully. Even in these days of publicity for auctions and TV programmes on collectibles, it is surprising what gets thrown into skips or disposed of in other ways. The public does not seem to associate value with anything that they might possess, perhaps a case of familiarity breeding contempt. I have occasionally bought extraordinary books from general dealers who have been *paid* to clear a house of its remaining contents. When my stepmother died, her executors called in a very knowledgeable valuer for probate. He valued an entire wall of books at four hundred pounds virtually without looking at them. When I queried this, he said that he only 'reckoned' fine leather books or old illustrated books, otherwise he always put such quantities of books in at four hundred pounds! I costed the lot, which I inherited anyway, at around two thousand pounds on a trade basis. It follows that good relations with valuers and solicitors are worth cultivating. I must have bid for dozens of executors' lots through the years, often by way of the solicitor, and on very few occasions have I been unsuccessful.

I have been dealing with what might be described as successful purchasing. In the early stages, until you get better known in an area or know better what to ask people on the phone, you will find yourself looking at batches of books which you definitely do not want to buy. Getting yourself out of such situations, which often occur at weekends or in the evening, since people work during the day, can be tricky and call for much tact. This is essential, despite the fact that you may be fuming at the waste of time and petrol involved. If you can't accustom yourself to it, just restrict yourself to buying from dealers and at book fairs, but remember that what you see will almost always have been picked over by other dealers with more experience than you. For fresh stock, it has to be the public.

When money does change hands, always clear the books straight away if you possibly can. This may mean taking boxes with you in case it rains, although with large cars like the Volvo it is possible to pack large quantities of books across the car in rows without damage to them. Obviously, one does have to come back sometimes, but it is best under those circumstances to pay when you collect. People change their minds, or decide to remove various items their family may take a fancy to, or even move if the house is for sale. Adjusting a price after you have paid can be very tricky.

BUYING IN THE TRADE

A very large proportion of all turnover in the book trade is between one dealer and another. It is not uncommon for a shop to do between sixty and seventy per cent of its business with the trade and the same proportion may well cover book fairs as a whole. I have long had a theory that the book trade is really fuelled by people like you bringing capital into it, but then I am a cynic. With catalogues the proportion will be lower, but still significant. It therefore follows that other dealers will do some of their trade with you and you should bear this in mind when dealing with them. I have said above that, whether you are at home or running a shop, you must get out and see what everyone else is doing. Keep mental notes of whatever you see and do not restrict yourself to your own areas of interest. If you want natural history, you may find it under natural history, but you may also find it under biography, travel, science, or even theology. If the dealer doesn't know what he is doing, you may find it in fiction or virtually anywhere. If you don't find natural history, you may well find another book priced at five pounds which you have seen elsewhere at fifty pounds. If you do, do bear in mind that the fifty pounds may well have been wrong, although the odds are that it is nearer the truth than the five pounds. Perhaps I should not have used that word 'truth': there is no absolute; a book is worth what it will fetch and it may be only worth that once. This is, however, one field where the impact of the Internet will be greatest, but you will have to refer to my coming section for that aspect of prices.

It is customary to reveal that you are a dealer when you enter a shop, perhaps presenting your card. Do not forget that you are likely to be paying with a business cheque, which will be unsupported by a bank card (which are not available for businesses). You should establish your credentials with the dealer. If you think you may not find anything, it is occasionally all right to look around a bit first and insert your card in a conspicuous way in the first book you pull out to buy. Whatever happens, you should not pull out a heap of books and *then* ask for trade terms. That is not correct trade etiquette. It may also cost you the offer of a cup of tea or coffee.

The matter of trade discounts can be variable. Recognised dealers get ten per cent, which is one of the reasons why you should declare yourself early on. If you want to negotiate more, that is up to you, but only do it for heavier items. I personally do not accept even the ten per cent unless I am spending ten pounds or more and I only ever make an offer if, for instance, it is something priced at forty pounds or more which I reckon has been there some time. Do not pile up a great heap, have it totalled and then ask for twenty per cent. That sort of discount is reasonably common in America but it is not so here. If you want to haggle about a lot of books, perhaps a whole section, leave them where they are while you talk about them. To take them off the shelf and upset the shop comes under the heading of undue pressure.

In book fairs you may put books underneath the stand with your card in and pay when you are ready to go or, if you are exhibiting, towards the end of the day. If you do that, it is, I repeat, quite unacceptable to seek to beat the seller down when you settle. He could have cleared the book at full price if you had not put it aside. If you forget to collect it, you must be prepared to pay the postage when it is sent on to you afterwards. Always do put a card inside – stallholders get jumpy after a bit if you don't.

You may find, when you order books by post, that you get asked for a credit-card number or cheque before it is sent. As you become better known and, above all, if you join the ABA or the PBFA, most books will be sent with an invoice. My policy is to ask for pre-payment from private customers or strangers and give credit only to the bona-fide trade or to institutions. You should hesitate to send money in advance to anyone who quotes you a book and who does not appear in the PBFA or ABA directories or at least in *Sheppard's*. It is by no means unknown for fly-by-night dealers to quote extremely attractive titles at low prices and then not to send the books. There is a great deal of trust in the book trade as a whole; foster it, do not abuse it.

PAYING FOR BOOKS

As for payment, except for a very few West End businesses, books bought at book fairs are normally paid for at the time of purchase. The same is true of purchases from bookshops, although, once you become known, it is possible to ask for thirty days' credit on large purchases. The rule of the trade associations is that one month's credit should normally be allowed to known dealers. On postal books, my habit (at least now) is that I pay for everything under twenty pounds by return of post after it has been collated; between twenty and forty pounds I try to pay within a fortnight; above forty pounds I pay at one month or when I receive the first statement. Sometimes I make arrangements for longer credit on substantial bills and I often take somewhat longer to pay for new books, which seems to be customary in that business.

It perhaps goes without saying in this business, as in most others, that frankness is essential if you find yourself in difficulties. If you have to delay payment, tell the other bookseller so and explain. People are very nice on the whole: it is silence they don't like. I still deal with several people who suffered a little when I ran into squally weather in the past. Their understanding helped me then and my continuing custom benefits them now. I am not advocating that you do this very often, of course, but you may find a trade creditor a good deal more understanding than a bank manager (or, nowadays, a bank computer).

There are, of course, other sources of books, notably the charity field, the Internet or jumble sales. Various booksellers I know have arrangements with their local charity sales to get in a day or two before the public. If you can get such a deal, you should not only spend fairly liberally but, if the books are priced, it is helpful to give more than the price marked, partly for goodwill and partly to assist the charity. At one large London event I tend to round a bill of one hundred and seventy-five pounds up to two hundred pounds, which has resulted in early entry for several years now.

In the early stages of your business, catalogues should be approached with caution as a source of books. If you have a narrow speciality, of course, you should buy almost anything that fits into your field if this is at all possible (see Chapter V Specialisations). If not, you should read the description carefully, perhaps check the book against one or two of the large sites on the Internet, and ask yourself quite realistically why you want the book and who might buy it from you. Some booksellers are very skilful writers of catalogue entries. It is, after all, their job. One pitfall is to think that a book priced at thirty-five pounds in a catalogue full of books priced between one hundred and one thousand pounds is a cheap book, whereas all it has is a cheap price for the company it is keeping. On a bookshop shelf, you might not look at it twice, or even think it overpriced. If you decide that, in your first few years, your means dictate that your general stock will be in the five to fifty pounds area, bar the odd coup, then acquire catalogues in that field. The expensive ones are always fun to look at, but do not approach them as potential sources of books, rather as sources of information for the future, when you may have worked up to that type of stock. I have found that small booksellers who are incessantly straining upwards when they cannot afford to tie up capital, or indeed have no spare capital, are riding for a fall.

If you look carefully at the stands in book fairs, you will find that the more conservative-looking dealers select what they buy and sell carefully, making sure that their stock is clean, well polished, if leatherbound, and well presented. Their stalls (and sometimes they themselves) may look rather dull, but they will be there long after the rip-roaring boys have made their fortunes (a tiny minority) or found themselves back at an office desk.

CHAPTER V

Specialisations

We are now beginning to get down to the nitty-gritty of this business if you are going to make anything of it. I have given some advice to those who are determined to run a shop, together with some warnings. I have covered some broad rules about general buying and selling of books. If you are trying to stretch a modest capital over a few initial years in the business, you cannot at the start ignore any source of profit and you would be unwise to cavil at the hard work involved in book fairs, in buying large quantities of books and at the evening and weekend work involved in buying books privately. Once you have got to grips with all of this, however, the question of specialisation must come up, even if only in parallel with the rest of your burgeoning business.

Before I deal with this subject, perhaps I should just pick up the term 'capital' from the last paragraph. Years ago, many of us used to say, "if only we had abundant capital, what hay we could make in second-hand and rare books!" Then one or two people surfaced who did have access to very major capital (Dr Nothmann of Covent Garden Books and David Brass of Joseph's spring to mind) and we discovered that it was not true. It is what you do with your resources that is important, not whether you command significant money. A book-trade commentator named Driff once published a cartoon of me which had me telling an apprentice bookseller that the way to deal with overdrafts was to 'transfer money from your private account'. It annoyed me mainly by being too close to the bone, but there is a general point there.

Many people in this business do have access to extra funds or to personal capital. I will assume that you do not, but you may be in competition with people who do.

Even to contemplate anything more ambitious than a part-time book career ancillary to another, main career, I think a sum of fifty thousand pounds is almost a minimum these days. It may be in the form of a bank overdraft, an additional mortgage, a retirement package or savings, but that kind of sum may well be absorbed in the first year or two, either in stock, living expenses or equipment (computers, etc.). I was on a train some years ago, talking to a number of quite well-known dealers and all of them had overdrafts in the sixty to a hundred-thousand-pound range and that may well have been in addition to their initial capital outlay. If the overdraft showed signs of getting much above that, they got alarmed, but they never quite seemed to get it to fall. They had all, I might add, had a fair amount to drink.

Let us return to specialisation. One friend of mine came out of the services and decided to go into bookselling. He asked an experienced bookseller what was the most unfashionable field at that time and the friend said 'Theology', so my friend went into that and, despite being an atheist, did very well for over thirty years. He was the exception that proves the rule. Whatever you choose, you should really have some kind of interest in it, if only to encourage you to know what is important and interesting and what is not. If your subject bores you, the odds are you will bore your customers. You don't have to be passionate about the subject, but you should have some intellectual curiosity about it. You are going, after all, to find yourself talking to intelligent collectors in your field at book fairs or on the phone. You might as well enter into it wholeheartedly.

WHAT LEVEL TO CHOOSE

Let us take a fairly straightforward subject, say cookery. You must decide your level and stick to it. One might call the choice rare, medium or well done. The rare bookseller will look for the scarce and early items and stick to those, producing catalogues which, by their feel and production, make it clear that, while he or she may deal with Delia Smith as a customer, they will not be stocking her books. As well as old books, such a dealer may look for important nine-teenth- and even twentieth-century books, fine menus, signed copies and manuscripts. If a valued customer asks for a modern standard cookery book, even if it is out of print, that dealer will recommend another, humbler denizen of the same field. Meanwhile, the 'rare' dealers will devote themselves to tracking down and cornering the rarities, building a reputation as the bookseller of last resort for the real collector. Such items and such catalogues will be expensive, but the dealer's time will go into the hunt for the book and the fine description of it when it has been found. Sales will be few in number but expensive. They are likely to avoid the complaint known to us as book-seller's back.

The 'well-done' person at the bottom aims to amass a large mailing list, lots of books in the field (sometimes new as well as secondhand books, certainly remainders) and a reputation for coming up with the goods. No title is too humble to go on their wants list and their lists of wanted books in *Bookdealer* will run to considerable length. Provided they have a good computer and a good memory, they will make up in customer loyalty and quantity sales what they lack in the rarities of cookery books. Some of their customers may buy original editions by Mrs Raffald, while others will be satisfied with later reprints. If they have time, they may get involved in discussions of recipes over the phone, but they won't have much time.

The 'medium' bookseller will come somewhere between the two. They may have a more in-depth stock than our first specimen, but they will avoid the sheer hard graft of the other. The books they deal with will be very out of print, rather than just out of print. They will say, when asked for a modern standard, that they really 'can't afford the time to deal with that type of book, which tends to crop up in jumble sales'. On the other hand, they may know all the ins and outs of Ambrose Heath titles (in dust wrappers, perhaps), whether there are scarce Elizabeth David titles and what they are, as well as the points related to early Mrs Beetons and the classic writers in the field.

TO FIRST OR NOT TO FIRST

For the more humdrum factual subjects, the example quoted above can be used as a template. If you have a spot of the Gerald Durrell in you, then natural history could be an obvious choice. If you cannot be an engine driver, you can at least deal in the memoirs of engine drivers, or books on the different kinds of GWR sorting yards. I came to specialisation fairly late in the day and went in for European travel for some years until the material became scarce, whereupon I did a smart move into European Royalty, a subject no one else took seriously. I am now in the process of starting a second string in British diarists, another neglected field. I have occasionally felt an inclination to go into wine books and I know excellent dealers in the music and theatre fields. Whatever you choose, go into even the cheaper books at a serious level, catalogue them properly, collate them at one level or another, pick up the expertise and treat the devoted collector as a serious customer – some of them may seem like nutters to you, but it takes all sorts...

It is when it comes to literature that the going gets muddy. There are probably more specialist booksellers in 'Eng. Lit.' than in anything else. It is an area of great expertise on points, where dust wrappers have developed into a cult, where the competition is fierce and the customers, although fairly plentiful, very choosy. It flourishes more in the US than it does in Britain, partly, I think, because there is a wider public for contemporary literature there. If you have a very good memory, it can be quite a cheap field to enter, since even paperbacks often have quite a significant value. Condition is of paramount importance, but I suppose it is of almost equal importance to appreciate what you are dealing with, i.e. to read the material. If you dealt in books on, say, medieval history, no one would expect you to have read all the key books – some of them, perhaps, but not all of them. But if you specialise in an area of fiction, you may well be expected to have read the texts. So don't go into it unless you like reading them.

There is, moreover, another drawback to this specialisation. In order to get a reasonable return on your work, you need to have a fair number of customers and a good mailing list for your catalogues. Each customer in modern literature, however, may well collect only one author. If that customer is on ten booksellers' mailing lists and 'his' author has written only thirty titles, he is rapidly going to be reduced to searching for a very few titles. If he is looking for, say, five books and is receiving, say, fifty catalogues annually, the chances of your selling him anything are pretty remote. Yet you may be mailing him and many another like him catalogues which have cost a deal to produce and not a negligible amount to mail. If you definitely want to go into this side of the business, I would suggest that you do not issue large catalogues. Issue small and tightly focused lists, perhaps by e-mail, giving almost a personalised service to the collector. When you find he has stopped buying, drop him.

Some years ago I started a book dealers' syndicate. This consisted of about forty booksellers who paid one-fortieth each of large advertisements in places like *The Economist* and the *New Yorker*, where individual dealers cannot normally afford advertisements. Potential customers could tick four of the specialities and the requisite dealers would send them their catalogues. It was a great success, although an enormous amount of work for my staff. Dealers who gave their specialities as 'First Editions' received hundreds of requests, but very few orders resulted. Those who narrowed the field did much better. One dealer who listed 'Churchilliana' had only fifty replies, but they proved a gold mine. On the other hand, although there are one or two dealers who deal in Churchill and nothing else, I think anyone specialising should have a field broad enough to keep selling to his better customers. If you decide on 'Tolkien', for instance, you will be constantly looking for new collectors as the old ones get saturated. I am myself finding this a little in the field of Royalty, large though it is: almost everyone I have been selling to for several years now has most of the better books.

KEEPING TABS ON YOUR FIELD

As you get further and further into your chosen field, you will wish to make sure you know what is going on there. Make sure you get your rivals' catalogues, if you have any rivals (a relative with a different name from yours living in a different part of the country may come in handy here). Run the basic titles you are always getting asked for through the search facility on the Internet and buy anything that is really under-priced. When you get further in, you could use the various facilities available for checking what is coming up at the major auction houses. A modest postal bid can ensure that, if it goes cheap, it will go to you. If it does not, then at least the value is seen to be maintained. Check all relevant titles at book fairs, keeping a check on what other dealers are asking for 'your' titles. Mop up anything that is seriously under your price if you can. If all this costs money, so be it, at least if you are building a business for the long term, although apropos this you might consider some remarks I shall be making shortly about reprints.

Let us examine this matter of stock in more detail. Say you specialise in travel books and you see a book you have priced at forty-five pounds in your stock. If it has been through one or two of your catalogues and is still unsold, take that into account. If the copy you see is a very good copy at twenty pounds, then clearly you should buy it. If it is thirty pounds, probably not. If your copy has not yet been through a catalogue, it might well be worth paying that thirty pounds (or twenty-seven pounds trade price). If you have three and you see two more in a book fair, you might seriously wonder whether your copies are over-priced. Go into the Internet and see what is to be found there. Oh dear, another fifteen copies ranging from seven pounds fifty to seventy-five pounds, with the mean around twenty-five pounds! You probably need to indulge in a spot of reassessment, although never, especially when you are getting more experienced, distrust a gut feeling that everyone else is wrong and it is you who are right. If you are knowledgeable and a sensible bookseller, stick to your guns, although a slight note under the next catalogue entry saying just why you think the book is important never comes amiss. When it comes to notes in catalogues, make up your own. There have been examples of explanatory notes which are wrong running for years through the trade as one dealer copies the catalogue of another. A knowledgeable specialist was telling me recently of a very valuable book which was always catalogued as 'lacking the rare extra leaf', simply because a bookseller before 1914 had mistakenly thought it did. No one had ever seen the leaf in question!

The above recipe for keeping up with your key books may sound complicated and it is, in fact, more intensive than it would have been a few years ago. The world is, however, getting more concentrated and you may well now be in direct competition with someone in the Middle West for the same customers. You must have the expertise if you are to make a success of your specialisation. Fortunately, much of the expertise can now be acquired through your computer keyboard. But not all; it remains important, where possible, to handle the actual books and to apply to them the knowledge culled from background reading round your subject. To hark back to the travel speciality mentioned above, anyone dealing in books on nineteenth-century African exploration must know the broad outlines of the history, its personalities and where their explorations and hence their books fit into the picture of the period. In that particular field, it may well be that the perspective on European explorers may change, and the demand with them.

DEAD SUBJECTS

Things do change in the book trade as in other businesses. For the first thirty years I was in the trade, there were several dealers who made a pretty good thing out of left-wing and Soviet studies, a subject which is largely dead now. Years later, when I bought the residual stock of the late Michael Katanka, it was crammed with books we would have given our back teeth for twenty years before but which were now dead in the water. A real bull market in Africana was largely killed by currency restrictions in South and East Africa in the 1970s and 1980s. For some thirty years after the war, teacher-training colleges and other libraries were moving heavily into sociology and allied subjects. In the past ten years many of these libraries have been closed and rationalised and the whole subject is a drug on the market. The principal dealer in it now specialises in finding specific books and newspapers to appear in TV and on film. Theatrical books do not seem to be what they were, but it has always been an ephemeral subject, and I have a feeling that natural history may be vulnerable to the CD-Rom. I do not, overall, think that CD-Roms are the threat to the book that some forecast. I feel fairly confident that the physical book will see me out, if that is any consolation to anyone, but one must not assume that demand will always attach to a particular subject. Sniff the wind and, if you don't like the way things are shaping, get ready to side-step smartly in some other direction.

There has been a scare lately about reprints, which is a subject I do know something about. There is a company in, I think, St Louis or somewhere like that which has apparently put loads of books on to the Internet. You pay and then print the book down. Over here, Macmillan have announced that they will be up-loading their whole back list and can reprint single copies to order. I took the trouble to discuss this with them and I think the threat is exaggerated. The basic charge is fifty pounds per book for a modest reprint, one-sided and without illustration, and perfect bound. This may be appropriate for technical works, but much of the Macmillan list is academic or literary and I am sure most people will continue to want a proper hardbound text through the secondhand market, where it will usually be cheaper as well. I will deal with this in more detail when looking to the future in my next part.

There is an opening for reprints and I think it may be more appropriate for our market to corner it rather than high-cost publishers. Where I think the average bookseller can take note is to remember something that many of us tend to forget: however important typefaces, dust wrappers, good bindings and first printings may be to us, a very high proportion of all books sold, be they new or used, are sold for one purpose, to be read. We forget that basic fact at our peril.

To get back to 'dead' subjects, the bookseller starting out on the second, or specialist phase of his bookselling would do well to consider where his speciality may be in ten years' time. It must take a minimum of about five years to get a good speciality established amongst the collecting community which will appreciate it. At the ten-year mark, the specialist may be at his peak in terms of market penetration, knowledge and profit. In this fast moving age, it is impossible to foresee exactly what may happen ten years hence, but it is worth thinking about. Twenty years ago a student with a degree in sociology who fancied selling books on it rather than practising in it himself might have thought that he was on to a permanently good thing. That is hindsight, but there are pointers. Clearly, the start of the new millennium is going to be dominated by screens of one sort or another. If there is one field that could benefit from that approach, it might be art reference. One could, of course, turn the argument on its head and say that a boom in art reference CD-Roms could stimulate interest in books on minor artists where no mass market will ever be possible. What is required is a little lateral thinking before you start.

To sum up, some kind of specialisation is probably essential, either as a main string or as a supplementary source of income. It should be something in which you have some kind of intellectual curiosity yourself. Once chosen, you must soak yourself in it and endeavour to become more knowledgeable in it than anyone else. Judge the level at which you intend to operate and direct all your buying to that end. Lastly, fine tune your service to your customers, be it by catalogue or by focused lists or even at book fairs, although I think that fairs are really for buying as far as specialists are concerned; it is not worth spending a thousand pounds or so on a stand at the June ABA Olympia Fair to add four or five names to your mailing list. There must be a better way of spending four days of your time, unless you are very confident that one of the other stands may exhibit a book so worthwhile as to render the whole operation profitable. That seems unlikely.

CHAPTER VI

Thoughts on Selling Books

Almost everything I have said thus far is, I hope, relevant to selling books, but it may be worthwhile to offer a few thoughts directly addressed to this subject. The title of this work emphasises *bookdealing for profit.* Pay no attention to those who say that I know nothing about this; whether I have succeeded or not, this has always been my aim and I have pursued it for forty years. In that period I have indeed turned over a great deal of money, made some profits and some losses and, tried to keep up with the changing scene. I must have something to impart.

One shop I control at present has done well, at least in book-trade terms. Baggins in Rochester is run by a conventional board of directors which meets regularly, prepares forecasts, monitors turnover minutely and is now, after a lot of fine tuning, doing rather well. I do not propose to analyse its running in detail, but the experience has reinforced an opinion I have had for some time that the financial side of bookshops follows roughly the same laws of economics as any other business. It is surprising how few booksellers appreciate this. It may be that, in my more hands-on operation in Ticehurst, I myself do not operate quite so tightly as the board forces me to do in Rochester, but I will leave that for discussion in my final chapter, which will be something of a challenge, since my publisher has suggested that I consider how a retiring bookseller should prepare for selling up! We will see how I rise to discussing that particular challenge.

It is extraordinarily easy to buy and sell books on a minute margin, in particular when you are dealing with friendly customers. Bear one fact in mind: your shop or your postal business has a breakeven point and your main aim is to get past that point. I have suggested that a breakeven point of over fifty thousand pounds is probably required, increased to perhaps seventy-five thousand pounds or so if you are going to remove a full-time, if modest, wage for yourself from the business. Under that level you may well be accumulating losses, although an increase in stock and only a gradual lift in your overdraft may conceal this fact for some time. Above that level, your gross and net margins tend to converge as you are tempted into more expensive books and your margins shrink: your increase in overheads should not keep pace with your increasing turnover. Once you have covered your fixed overheads, you only have to retain your margin to turn a profit.

We will assume that the prices at which you buy do allow of a profit. If you have a shop, as I have explained, you will need to keep your stock moving by getting out and about, displaying it properly, dusting it occasionally and making some effort to be helpful to your customers. I have always found a fairly high profile in the local community helps you get known and certainly you should make efforts to get into the local paper, which often has trouble filling the space between the advertisements.

I should take a fairly cautious approach to advertising. Classified advertisements are worthwhile over a long period – use the cheap drip method. *Yellow Pages* are as useful as anything for buying. Display advertising is expensive and usually has little effect. Two hundred pounds or so does not go very far, even locally, while several hundreds can be required to make any impact in a national paper for one day. It is editorial cover that is really worthwhile, so try to get in any coverage of your area, even to the extent of buying journalists drinks. If you buy or sell anything newsworthy, issue some kind of press release about it. When you join a trade association, keep them posted on your activities. They may help you with national publicity.

You are on better ground with specialisation. Most such areas have magazines devoted to them and these will be read by people on exactly your wavelength. If you deal in militaria, get into the magazines closest to that field. A small advertisement in every issue of one such magazine is a good buy. There are loads of serious small magazines attached to old regimental associations, for instance, although they don't all take advertisements. Sometimes they will write you up for nothing. You should certainly ensure that all book-trade magazines carry wants lists from you so that the rest of the trade knows your specialities. You should also make sure that the various trade directories cover you: get the entries back in good time and go into as much detail as they will allow. If there are specialist book fairs in your field, which is possible but somewhat unlikely, travel long distances to them, for their customers are the ones you want.

MAILING LISTS

As you become better known, you will acquire names and addresses of those interested in your subject. The usual next step has been to prepare catalogues of gradually increasing sophistication and send them to these customers, plus perhaps rival dealers and libraries and other institutions. It is worth making some effort with non-trade bodies to make sure that the catalogue gets into the right hands. Phone them up and ask who is in charge of the library, or that section of the library or faculty concerned with your subject. A personally addressed catalogue is much less likely to end up in a secretary's wastepaper basket. The present craze for junk mail has not helped the book trade.

But note my hedging phrase above: 'the usual next step has been'. I am not so sure now that this is quite such plain sailing. It may be that a venture on to a web site should come next, followed by a limited e-mailing to those who have bought books from you. Again, beware of creating the impression of junk mail. A two-page conventionally catalogued list sent to, say, twenty e-mail addresses with tightly focused books should be both cheap and effective. It may be that a succession of these will keep the money flowing and that, every so often, you can reorganise the books left unsold into a larger list to be sent by mail. This has the smack of a two-class system between those who are on line and those who are not, but it may be the way the world is going. Further down the line still, a stocklist consisting of several hundred titles in your speciality could be on the cards, but not every bookdealer will wish to enter his field in quite such depth. I have found it extraordinarily useful in my Royalty field.

To produce the catalogue, there is no question of using anything but a computer these days. Small runs can perhaps still be printed in-house on a laser printer or copier, but there are several specialist catalogue printers advertising in the book-trade press who produce quite lengthy catalogues at surprisingly low prices. It is probably better to go with them. Most of them will print from your copy, from disc or from CD.

How many successive catalogues should you send? This is one of the great imponderables of the trade. Some, like Graham Weiner the scientific bookseller, go on sending for ages and then are pleasantly surprised to receive a large order from a hitherto moribund customer. This may be worthwhile with libraries, but I think private customers should be given only so much rope. If they lose interest or move or die, you are rarely notified. I would have thought that four catalogues after the last order is getting near the end. A note inside the final one sent asking for confirmation of interest in continuing seems a polite way of dealing with the matter. (If it is you who are the customer and you wish to continue to receive the catalogues without necessarily spending much, order an expensive but slightly underpriced book a month after you receive the catalogue. You won't get the book, but you will go on receiving the catalogues.) With some booksellers I have found that the problem is not staying on the list but getting off it; they seem to have no real contact with their mailing lists.

Northcliffe, I think it was, said that half of all advertising was wasted, but you never knew which half. I would put it at a good deal more than that, but the principle underlying the remark was sound. With catalogues, about ninety per cent of all the orders come from about ten per cent of the customers, but that ten per cent may differ from catalogue to catalogue. None the less, this is quite an expensive way of selling and a sharp eye needs to be kept upon your printing and postage costs. I know at least one dealer who thinks that shedding ninety per cent of his mailing list would barely affect his takings, but he could not justify producing a catalogue for as few as fifty remaining customers. Clearly he should now be looking at the e-mail option. We all like the feeling of being in touch with quantities of potential buyers, but make sure the whole operation is at their expense and not at yours.

LEARNING FROM BOOK FAIRS

In the matter of selling books, your attendance at book fairs, at least in the early stages, is crucial. I would really recommend you to exhibit at some, but even if you don't there is something to be said for 'casing' the fair properly. Try it with two of the three monthly Bloomsbury fairs, for instance. The HD one at the Royal National kicks off around 10.00 a.m. on the Sunday and the main PBFA Fair at the Russell at 1.00 p.m. The second PBFA fair is proving very popular. It is my purely personal view that this Post House Fair will do much more harm to the fair at the Russell than it will to the HD Fair. This is not because I myself exhibit at the latter, but because there is a much more disparate selection of stock at the HD Fair, while the Post House is similar to its sister fair but more convenient, being only for one day instead of for two. It is almost impossible to examine all three fairs thoroughly in the time available. Something will have to give. As far as you can, do them in turn, watching to see how busy they are and what gaps are appearing where. Then do them again, the Royal National between 4.00 p.m. and 5.00 p.m. before it closes and then the Russell again around 6.00 p.m. See whether things have gone slack, see which dealers have large gaps and try to work out why and, observe their demeanours. I have found that, with many stallholders, they will say they are having a rather good day, although last month was pretty awful; they will say the same next month!

Some of the takes in such fairs can be very low, judging by the published averages, and you are trying to find out why. Quite a lot of dealers simply repeat a large proportion of their stock every month, just filling up the gaps. Others, as I have already remarked, appear to make no effort to polish or even dust their books. This may have something to do with the fact that quite a number of the ones involved in these fairs are part-timers. Their time for acquiring stock is limited. Another reason is that some of them are basically lazy. It is quite easy to spot the energetic, intellectually active ones amongst them and these are worth studying. Unfortunately, they are often not at their own stalls since they are busy buying from other dealers. The London fairs and some of the provincial ones are little worlds of their own, a little too introverted in my view. The gossip and the drinks seem to take precedence over the business, although this is common to many trades. Always remember that the books on the shelves have not been sold. Some of the best ones may not even be there since the dealer has not recognised their importance. Treat published turnover figures with caution, be they from the ABA or the PBFA. The larger fairs may see some ironing out through the averaging but on the whole a good buy will produce a good take, and vice versa. In the early stages, you can learn most from the Royal National and the Russell each month, the ABA Chelsea Fair in the autumn and the larger PBFA fairs in the provinces. Further down the scale, it is well worth visiting non-association fairs hunting for bargains and you will, of course, have to exhibit at them yourself until you qualify for membership of the two associations.

Very few booksellers spend much on binding, which I think is a pity. It is now very expensive to get books leather-bound and you must be very sure of your market before you spend fifty or sixty pounds on a new half-leather binding. On the other hand, a cloth binding put on to a book acquired cheaply because of its poor covers can often be well worth the price. Look carefully around your home area to see if you can come up with a reasonable binder. Try to find someone who has what I term a 'journeyman' outlook rather than a potential fine binder. You want someone who appreciates that you have to price the book realistically after it has been bound. They are hard but not impossible to find.

As for keeping track on book lots, I have seen many booksellers work out the most elaborate systems of codes to enable him to tell just when a particular book lot has paid for itself. A code goes into each book to show what it has cost (which, with a large lot, is pretty much guesswork). When the book is sold, the bookseller solemnly copies the code into his cash book and, I imagine, transfers it into another book with its fellows from the same lot afterwards. Eventually, by adding it all up, one can discover that you paid a hundred pounds for a lot, took a hundred and twenty pounds in the first month, forty-five pounds in the second and eventually showed a good return, even allowing for the unsold residue. I wonder whether anyone really keeps the whole system up for long? It all seems designed to take up time which could be devoted to cleaning, collating or buying books. At the risk of offending some people, I think it is essentially a small-time approach to dealing.

BASIC COSTING

Where it is vital to keep some check is when you buy a lot. Until you learn to trust your own judgement, you should sit right down with a duster and a pencil and price the whole lot. On cheap books (i.e. an average unit price of seven pounds fifty or less), you should look to triple the price paid or better. Leave out the paperbacks altogether and cost books which need binding in at nothing unless they are potentially very good. Obviously the mark-up will fall as the average price rises. When you have a really good lot, which presumably will be rather small in numbers, it might average out at twenty-five or even fifty pounds per book and with that lot you might expect to have doubled your purchase price, or, if they are quick sellers, paid an even higher proportion. And so on upwards. If you have tripled your money on a private lot of very expensive books, you have probably 'done' someone, let us hope inadvertently. Do not suffer unduly if you feel you have, for it takes time to cost a lot properly in someone's house; but try not to do it too often, for it will eventually result in a poor reputation and fewer books.

You may think that all this should have been done before you bought the books. Maybe, but the actual situation rarely works like that. You will usually be left in a room with the books for a certain period and you will scribble bits and pieces of prices on a piece of paper, rounding it up or down as the mood takes you. Mood, in fact, has a lot to do with it. I usually say that a figure comes into my mind after a bit and I then adjust it up or down as I go on through. It is not usually practicable to sit down and go through every book with a calculator at your elbow. Apart from the look of the thing, the odds are that you are sipping a cup of coffee and listening to the owner tell you about where they are moving to at the same time. Hence the importance of checking up when you get the books back. That figure that comes into your head should be refined each time so that after a period it becomes almost infallible. The information stored in your mind from all the bookshops and book fairs you have seen must correlate with the books you are viewing so that your eye slides over the common books and picks out the rare and interesting ones almost as second nature.

Once this method of buying private books becomes ingrained in you, the pricing of them becomes almost second nature. If the total on the lot comes to less than you had expected, try to resist going through it again and pushing the prices up to compensate. That is the wrong reason for increasing a price. Now that you have the cross-checking facilities of the Internet available to you, it may be that you will wish to pull out the best ten per cent of the lot and see whether your prices fit in with the (still fallible) figures which come up on the screen. It is at this point that it may be possible to up some of your prices, but then you may find yourself bringing some down. Progressively, however, you must learn to trust your instincts and your growing experience in pricing. There is, as I have said, no absolute: if you feel you can achieve a certain price, then that is the price, whatever the Internet or other people's catalogues may say. If you are consistently wrong over this, you probably won't last anyway.

THE BEST BOOKS

If you are doing well from your buying, your fairs, your catalogues of one sort or another and your specialisations, it may be that you wish to consider dealing in rarer books eventually. If you can afford it, and only if, this is the point at which you may decide to channel a few of the best books you buy into a kind of reserve stock against that day. Rather than simply go for the best of everything, you should bear in mind what this is for: is it to give you a sound stock upon which to base eventual entry into the ABA, so that you can exhibit well at a really good fair, or is it to form the basis of a rare specialist stock? When you have progressed some way, bear in mind one salient fact. Many a bookseller has sprung a really good stock on a wondering trade and public, one that has taken him or her years to accumulate, only to find that the books sell quickly and cannot be replaced at the same level. Think long term at all times (provided, of course, that you do want to remain in the business long term). The time that goes into private buying when you have another job tends not to get costed into the prices of any starting stock, whereas replacements inevitably do include time, whether formally or not.

When you do allow your reserve to surface, that is the time to push the prices upwards, always provided that the books you have stockpiled are, at second or third viewing, good books. Get a healthy price for them or hang on to them, for that money is going to have to be used to replace them. You are fortunate to be starting at a time when inflation is controlled, so you are not faced with every book you buy being more expensive than its predecessor, as was the case for some years. Better books, however, do become scarcer as time goes on and, in particular, your own specialist books may well increase in price because of your own proselytising efforts. In my younger years there was a British topography dealer called Stanley Crowe, a charming man, who dominated the market in that subject. Prices in it have never been quite the same since he died. Ben Weinreb 'made' the market in architectural books, but in his case he had disciples who carried on the good work. A fine dealer in a particular field commands prices and, if you have a real flair for a subject, there is no reason why you should not do so as well. On the other hand, there have been dealers like Bernard Simpson who squirreled away fine books for their old age, only to find that the taste had changed when they came to sell. There is such a thing as being too long term. There is no reason to believe that books will necessarily advance in value in line with interest rates or our lower rates of inflation; they never did in the twentieth century.

As you move up the trade, certain stages will have to be gone through. You will be expected to stock the standard 'heavy' books in your field and these will cost money, money which may be tied up for long periods. This may need extra capital or loans, which have to be anticipated. If it looks as if capital will remain tight, continue parallel dealing in general books and do not be too proud to continue selling at routine book fairs, for cash flow is always going to be important. You may also be approached for 'arrangements' of one sort or another. Keep well clear of anything that smells like a ring. You may also be asked, however, to lend books to other dealers for offering to their customers, or even for display in their shops. Assess your potential temporary partner quite dispassionately, sticking if possible to fellow members of your trade association, which gives you a comeback if things go wrong. Get some kind of written confirmation of terms, especially as regards time limits. You may also get offers of joint purchasing where an item is too expensive for one dealer to handle. I think we are now moving out of the scope of this book, but be careful. If your gut feeling is against any suggested deal, keep clear of it however much you are assured that 'everyone does it' in the trade. They probably don't.

CHAPTER VII

Cataloguing and Other Pitfalls

I do not propose to append much of a list of booksellers' abbreviations to this book, as I warned in my Preface. I would certainly suggest that the aspiring bookseller examine carefully every decent catalogue he can lay hands on. That is not difficult, incidentally, for most established booksellers have stacks of outdated catalogues from other dealers which can be had for the taking. The entries on ABE and others sites on the Internet should also be scrutinised and there are, of course, actual reference lists available. *The Clique* of York have recently issued a CD-Rom containing ten years of catalogue entries from the middle of the trade, some two hundred and fifty thousand entries for eighty pounds, which is worth buying. There is a very good guide each year in the *ABA Handbook*, although the beginner might be well advised to take some of the admonitions there with a pinch of salt. It can be picked up for nothing at ABA Fairs or sent on demand from their office.

Above all, however, the beginner has one great advantage over someone of long experience like myself. He brings to cataloguing an outside mind uncluttered by the bibliophily ingrained in us. If you don't understand what is meant, you can look it up for curiosity's sake, but why adopt it? If you don't understand, then most of your potential customers won't either. You have to evolve and, if necessary, invent a way of explaining your offering to the potential buyer.

A LAY MARKET

This is the last chapter in this section and the one in which I am going to advance some really heretical views. Towards the end of this book there will be a short example of cataloguing without abbreviations. Depending on your market, try to use as few abbreviations as possible. Since the growth of Internet bookselling, it is already noticeable that many are on the way out and the reason is simple – booksellers have realised that the public to whom they are talking simply doesn't understand them. When you reach the dizzy heights of rare specialist cataloguing, by all means cater to the committed and experienced collector, but until then assume that you are writing for the general public. If the new departures are worth anything, it is to bring fresh buyers into our market. Many of them will not, in this day and age, like to feel that they have to have a course first before they can understand our listings. I have had quite established customers who have been unable to understand Roman pagination and unaware of what the abbreviation 'pp' signifies, let alone what the abbreviation 'ffep.' is about, and all this long before they try to disentangle the different Latin words used by booksellers to describe the sizes of book they are advertising. For goodness sake, we are trying to sell something, not get one up on the customer! I have known booksellers who think that anyone who cannot disentangle a high-flown book description does not really deserve to have the book. There is, of course, nothing shaming in someone not understanding what we are talking about. We would probably not understand the patois of their business either.

The word octavo is probably useful and I have in the past printed in catalogues by the way of explanation that 'octavo is the size of a normal hardback'. Many amateurs will be quite happy with expressions like 'large' or 'small' octavo, even if this moves away from accepted trade custom. It is also probably permissible to use quarto and folio, with variants of them – although I mentioned the word quarto to an experienced modern printer of about thirty-five years of age the other day and he had never heard it. Many booksellers are now moving over to noting actual dimensions, although one wants to distinguish here between metric and imperial measurements, since the crucial American market does not take kindly to the former. When you are dealing with some series it is also possible to assume that the prospective customer knows what you are writing about: if a customer does not know what size a *Baedeker* or an *Almanach de Gotha* is, he or she is unlikely to want to pay heavily for the one you are offering. You might even be able to get away with describing it as 'in the usual binding', but don't push your luck on that sort of thing. Beyond these narrow confines, it is always better to assume that the customer is unfamiliar with what you are describing, putting things in simple and transparent terms. Always distinguish between paper-covered and hardbacked books, describing as nearly as you can the appearance of the book. I have already emphasised the necessity to under-describe, but I will repeat it here. No one ever complained because a book was better than he or she expected.

Tell them how many pages there are, what sort of illustrations the book has and, particularly with older books, check that the illustrations are actually there. It is now more or less accepted that small ownership signatures need not be described (except in the modern first edition market), but certainly anything large or disfiguring should be carefully noted. The place of publication, the publisher and the date should follow. It is surprising how often the publisher is omitted.

Unless relevant, there is normally no need to say a book is a first edition, for most are. This definitely does not apply to anything in the literary or fiction fields, where edition may be everything. If you do propose to sell modern firsts (and an uncomfortable number of potential booksellers do), there may well be something to be said for going on some kind of course in the recognition of what are called 'points', the often minute differences between various editions. There are reference works to be had on how to recognise a first edition, highlighting the variations between publishers' customs. Never put a really fancy price on what you think is a modern first edition without first checking the Internet, plus one of the price reference books, the Michael Coles's CD-Rom or a specialist catalogue. It is fatally easy to get these things wrong and damage your credibility.

Assuming that most of your cataloguing, at least in the initial stages, comprises general works outside the first editions market, there are certain other common-sense rules to apply. If the title itself does not give a fairly thorough clue to what the book is about, tell the customer in a note. Look at the way books are explained in other people's catalogues and adopt their habits if they seem sensible, which usually means whether they make the description more comprehensible. Far too many catalogues are a kind of plot between bookseller and experienced customer to ensure that anyone outside the field has no idea what is going on (a trait they have in common with most up-market auction catalogues). It is, however, a melancholy fact that the number of serious collectors has been falling for years, a decline which you and I are striving to reverse. I believe that many potential collectors are put off by too much perceived expertise. Two years ago we had a furious battle at the ABA to move our main June Book fair from Grosvenor House, an obvious up-market and élite venue, to Olympia, a very much more run-of-the-mill exhibition space. That move was a triumphant success, attracting people who would not have ventured across the threshold at Grosvenor House. That philosophy does not yet permeate much of the top of the trade, but it should.

There is, of course, a snobbery about how scarce or rare a book may be, let alone whether it is 'common' or, horror of horrors, 'a reading copy'. This last expression makes us appear ridiculous, for what is a book for, if not for reading. I have been finally cured of that particular snobbery by listening to buyers in my vast Baggins shop in Rochester enthusing over books in a condition in which I would in the past have consigned them to a skip. It is important that a shop look clean and tidy, but really enthusiastic customers often view things a little differently.

Remember that, as time goes on, you will see many more secondhand books than any customer. I have occasionally pulled myself up after saying, "Oh, that's a very common book", in the realisation that I may have seen ten copies of it in three years amongst perhaps a million books viewed. Books and the perception of them change. I used at one time to sneer at any shop which priced Nansen's *Farthest North* highly. It is now highly prized and justifiably so. With the possible exception of that beautiful Shell book called *The Scallop*, almost anything can come into fashion. When I was first in the trade, the ultimate insult for any book was to call it 'Victorian'.

WHAT IS ACCEPTABLE?

How should one progress up the cataloguing tree? Until recently, one started with a manual typewriter and a copying machine, not a modern copying machine but a Gestetner or Roneo machine which produced a limited number of what were usually very unsatisfactory lists which one stapled together and sent out to anyone who might be interested in your books. One progressed from there to using small printers and eventually to an altogether glossier production. I have already recommended some of the small printers who offer booksellers reasonably priced and well-produced printed catalogues in the pages of *Bookdealer*. Postage is also very expensive these days, however, so one should always ask oneself what one is trying to do and who are the customers. There is that saying that one sells ninety per cent of the books to ten per cent of the mailing list. That may be an exaggeration; for one thing one is quite lucky to sell ninety per cent of the catalogue at all. It is fatally easy, however, to accumulate names and addresses to feed the ego rather than the bank balance. Be pretty ruthless about cutting people off your lists.

You might also think quite hard before putting them on in the first place – for instance, if you are a general bookseller and someone sends you a well-judged letter explaining that they collect, say, Graham Greene. You may put the odd one in your catalogues, but the odds are that he has most of the usual ones already. If you get something really scarce, it is just as easy to drop a card to one of the specialists in the field and sell it for the price of a postcard. Very few customers, in my experience, tell you to stop sending catalogues and you may waste ten or even twenty pounds on a collector where your chances of any kind of return are minimal. This is, of course, a further reason for specialisation, although even there one has to refurbish the mailing list constantly as collectors either acquire most of the works in their field or even change their collecting interests.

I am coming to the conclusion nowadays that the day of the broad-based catalogue is passing. How much easier it is to restrict oneself to serious customers, find out their wants in depth and then mail or e-mail them a small list every so often. It is not so satisfying as is the production of a swanky catalogue with several hundred items in it, but it is almost certainly more profitable. A list of thirty nicely selected items sent to ten customers every couple of months will yield a good take in proportion to the work and cost involved. Multiply that, cultivating (say) sixteen separate batches of customers at the rate of two batches a week and constantly reviewing what is a practical number, and you have the makings of a business. You may get fifty orders for your thirty books, or rather fifty spread over twenty of them; the duplicate orders are used to build your wants list and you effectively go on selling off that small list for a year or two. I now insist on all our dealings and transactions with each customer being noted on the back of a file card (much easier than a computer list) so that anyone answering the telephone knows straight away what the customer has had and when, how well they pay, if one has written to them lately and as much else about them as possible. They are your kitchen garden and they need constant hoeing and perhaps also weeding, if that is not pushing the metaphor too far.

I have myself gone down a slightly different path on cataloguing. I do put out very substantial catalogues occasionally, almost more like reference books, but in the main I put my catalogues inside the magazines I produce. My main speciality is books on European Royalty and we produce the standard monthly magazine in the field, with an eight-page catalogue of new and old books inset. In that way the weeding is done automatically, for those who lose interest simply don't renew their subscriptions. If people will pay a subscription for a catalogue or a magazine, you know that they are, at least superficially, serious about the subject. It is a good deal too easy to send a postcard or a letter to a catalogue bookseller and enjoy a whole run of catalogues for nothing. Producing magazines is, of course, capital intensive and I suspect that most specialists, unless they confine themselves in the future to the Internet, will increasingly concentrate on small, tightly focused lists sent by e-mail.

GRASPING CHANGE

Much of what I have discussed in this book so far comes under the heading of looking backwards, which is why I have used the somewhat brutal part heading LATE TWENTIETH CENTURY to cover these chapters. Much of my forty years in the trade is covered by this material, although I have deliberately omitted most of my usual anecdotes concerning dusty days in large country bookshops happily turning over tens of thousands of volumes. Most of the bookshops tucked into my memory have now gone and the ones still left tend to be much smaller and more knowing. The rise of the book fair introduced a lot of smaller booksellers to a much wider market and prices have been to some extent ironed out. Miscellaneous lots at auction are less common and sellers of larger libraries have been seduced away to the major auction houses, largely because a generation of booksellers before the war were too unsure of themselves and too short of capital to build and safeguard a reputation for giving fair prices. The auction houses themselves, after a golden age from around 1960 to 1995, are under severe attack from on-line auctions and other developments.

The auctioneers will have to cope with their own problems; what I am concerned with is the survival of the small bookseller. As with the small grocer, the small any trader, we will survive by combining use of all the new developments with an attention to detail, a good background knowledge and good service based on high moral standards. Almost anyone can now buy a load of books at auction, sign on to a book-service provider on the Internet and set up in business. But that will not make them a proper bookseller and they will not last the course. As this book goes to press, the dot.com frenzy seems to have spent itself and a good job too. I shall devote the rest of this short book to some thoughts on how I see the trade developing in the next few years. I do not think we will be outdated by books on demand or CD-Roms, except perhaps in the reference-book field. The handheld, decently printed and easily read book will have its place in our civilisation for decades to come yet. Customers will be out there, but they must value the service they are being given. The increase in the price of secondhand books has for years been falling behind inflation, which is the greatest single reason for the decay of the secondhand bookshop. We will have to adapt our practices and our prejudices to survive.

Part II

Early Twenty-First Century

Chapter VIII

A Rapidly Changing Business

The idea of this second part is not simply to adapt the techniques sketched out in the previous portion of the book so as to take some account of changing technologies. It is rather to examine the future of the book as a whole, where the 'new' bookselling may be going, and what relationship secondhand or used books may have to these changes – indeed, whether secondhand bookselling does have a future.

The average bookdealer, in my experience, may have become reasonably familiar with the Internet and with e-mails, but he or she has yet to think through the possible impact of 'books on demand' and of the revolution that has taken place in reprinting, let alone the more long-term future of the Internet. As I write, the globalisation of technology means that an emerging country with very low wages can produce workers and printing machinery (to use a word which may itself be becoming dated) which rival anything in the first world.

FUTURE OF THE BOOK

It is, of course, impossible to be categorical about whether the printed book has a future. One simply has to take a position based on what information one has and argue from that. It is my view, after reading a great deal of speculative writing on the subject, that the printed book will last another fifty years at least. If books were to be fated to die in the blizzard of modern technology, it is unreasonable to suppose that a large market will arise in old books as curios of the past. A small market, perhaps, but nothing along present lines. If new books stopped being produced, there would be progressive destruction of past books and persons desirous of information would switch to the new means of communication. The fate of the book would be like that of the 78 rpm record, where the major saveable content has been transferred to CD or tape.

My feeling is that one only has to postulate such an eventuality to realise how very far we are from that position now. We in this country currently publish more books than ever before. The CD-Rom, which was the darling of the *Bookseller* magazine a few years ago, has consolidated its position as a business and reference tool, but it has conspicuously failed to take off as a mass-market product. Information has moved on-line, but in a fragmented and decidedly user *un*friendly way. The *Encyclopaedia Britannica* may have gone the way of all flesh and transferred itself to CD-Rom, but that is the exception – even most smaller reference books are being produced in book form in unprecedented numbers. For sheer convenience, the printed book has not yet shown any signs of being outdated. Even in terms of time, one would need a computer constantly on-line, free to use and probably voice activated to come anywhere near the speed with which it is possible to look up information in a book. I am not saying that such tools are not convenient for education. Clearly it is a fantastic thing to look up a planet on the appropriate site and see the planets turning in their spheres, hear commentary and zoom in on interplanetary travel, or to see a bird's bone structure, listen to its call and watch it build a nest. Most books are not, however, used for these purposes. Fiction remains the most popular subject matter, but biographies are also better researched and better written than they have ever been and the same applies across the board. At a basic level, I may use a spellchecker on this text, but for meanings and nuances I go to books.

Enough of this argument, which can be made to go on and on. Let us simply accept a basic premise that the printed book is far from dead and work on from there. As I have already mentioned, the great scare recently has been that the customer may soon be able to walk into a 'bookshop', order any book and watch it being printed and bound in front of him or her, a one-off reprint. There have been announcements along these lines from various UK publishers and from some specialist firms in the US. I have followed up one or two of them and they seem to have three drawbacks:

- they are very expensive per copy
- the printing and binding is poor, and
- very few people have found it worthwhile to make the significant investment involved. Some might find my comment that printing and binding is poor a little odd, but look at the quality of the average e-mail – unjustified, no italics or other refinements and produced in a standard typeface. The books will, it seems, be perfect bound and printed on one side of the page only. When I last enquired, prices started at fifty pounds per book. There is also some doubt at to whether, barring perhaps academic texts, the market in second-hand books is large enough to justify the considerable investment demanded.

Curiously enough, efforts are constantly being made to extend the efficiency of locating and buying secondhand books, not least through the Internet, and this is producing lower prices. Running through the offerings of a site like ABE, for instance, no one can say that the market for used books is stagnating, even if one did not know that the single most prominent product in the Internet age has turned out to be new books. It is, however, a fragmented market, spread over millions of possible titles. While the levelling down of prices has its drawbacks for the used-book dealer, there is no denying that it makes the task of the one-off re-printer a good deal harder. My feeling is that this is a red herring, since it is now possible to print an edition of, say, twenty-five copies of an out-of-print book at a price which knocks the one-off into a cocked hat. It is in the small-run reprinting world that developments will occur and I will deal with this aspect at some length.

THE AMAZONS OF THIS NEW WORLD

While we are looking at the present and future of the book, it might be an idea to consider the major on-line new booksellers. Amazon has yet to make a profit, although its losses have probably been exaggerated by adding in the written-off goodwill of companies the company has taken over. None-the-less, it is naive to think that simply cutting out the shopkeeper leads to immense savings. Amazon still has stocking and warehousing costs, let alone packing. It has become accepted recently that the firm makes a loss of five dollars on every book sold. This is excused because the management is said to be after market share, lists of buyers and general goodwill so that other products can be added to the range, which will eventually generate profits by sheer volume. This may turn out to be true, although I have my doubts, but it assumes that Amazon's future is not really simply as a bookseller but as a general retailer.

The likes of Blackwell's, W.H. Smith and Waterstone's are now moving into the Internet in a big way and it is there that the major expansion of on-line bookselling in Britain will eventually take place. In other words, this will be traditional bookselling adapted to the new technology. I don't find that frightening. What is interesting is that it has coincided with the collapse of the Net Book Agreement in the United Kingdom, although not yet on the Continent. The latter is only a matter of time, given the global nature of the Internet. It is only ring-fenced language markets which are keeping price maintenance alive outside English-language markets now. The price cutting which has followed the collapse of the NBA led the chains to over-expand and there is likely to be a drastic shrinkage shortly, with an attempt to build up Internet sales as a counterbalance.

There is a growing knock-on effect into the second-hand trade in all this. The so-called 'Recommended Retail Price' is being ignored, discounts from publishers are increasing, price cutting pushes the real prices of popular titles down, while in academic publishing sales languish, printing runs are cut and prices rise. The shelf life of a published book constantly diminishes and remaindering undercuts the reader's confidence in published prices. Save in certain narrow first-edition fields, hardback fiction prices in the secondhand market have already collapsed and publishers show signs of abandoning initial publication in hardback, which may undermine the first-edition market, perhaps the most successful used book field of the past twenty years. Publishers of non-fiction are constantly seeking cheaper printing overseas, but published prices do not fall – it is margins that rise and discounts that widen. Many quite significant books are now published in boards rather than cloth and a further move into initial publication in paperback seems inevitable in the non-fiction area as well. These latter developments have implications for secondhand books in that paperbacks and even to some extent boards have a shorter life than clothbound or leather books. This could, of course, be turned to account by pricing up those less durable books that do survive.

I have been dealing recently with a major publisher with a presence both in the UK and America and their attitude was that it was hardly worth publishing a title in both places since customers on the other side would order the original publication through the Internet. This may be an over-reaction, but it shows the way the wind is blowing. The idea that there are any practicable walls between various English-language markets is dated.

POLARISATION AMONGST NEW BOOKS

To summarise, I think the book as a medium of communication is reasonably safe. Where I have doubts is in the future flow of ex-new books into the secondhand market. There is already a certain sameness about much of the stock in book fairs and secondhand bookshops. It is notably easier to buy titles from the inter-war years than from the thirty years after 1945. Partly this is to do with paper rationing, but it also has something to do with smaller editions, many of which went into libraries and never came out, the rise of the (disposable) paperback and, in more recent years, the inflation of book prices, which, between 1960 and 1990, rose considerably faster than inflation. When I was last briefly in publishing many years ago, it used to be said that, leaving library sales aside, a third of all serious new books in the United Kingdom were sold by three (or was it four?) bookshops in Central London. Outside Central London, serious buyers of hardbacks are thin on the ground – except, of course, at Christmas, the season by which bookshops live and die, but that is largely a particular type of book. No one is ever going to get rich on secondhand Delia Smith books.

I probably see as many books for sale in private houses as most booksellers and, while I buy and sell in a fairly affluent area, the standard of books is depressing. The good 'collections' almost always come from older families and date back decades. The average person under sixty selling their own rather than their family's books, usually because they are moving somewhere smaller, has a pretty mediocre lot of books. One comes across the odd specialist, the archaeologist or local historian who still thinks in terms of *owning* the books they use, but they are scarce and getting scarcer. Even dons, who are not quite as hard up as they like to make out, seem to think in terms of recommending their college or university libraries to acquire the books they want – they don't seem to think in terms of buying them for themselves any more.

Likewise the comprehensive collector seems to be fading away, perhaps tempted into more tactile fields. I used to have a scattering of customers who would buy anything in their field they did not already own. Such customers are most uncommon now, in fact I hardly know any outside the semi-professional bookselling field. I might perhaps exclude the real antiquarian collector from this sweeping statement. Clearly a collector of Milton is not going to shy away from anything as long as he can afford it, although he may draw a date line. The trickle of persistent customers who once collected *every* edition of *Omar Khayyam*, or *anything* on West Country railways, or any Foulis Press printing – they and their ilk seem to be a dying breed.

THE NON-BOOK

If one-off printing has a limited future until much greater strides in technology come forward (and cheap technology at that), the alternative excitement seems to be the complete departure from the printed word. The hand- or desk-held rechargeable device with a screen is attracting much attention among publishers. It may soon be possible, upon payment of a fee, to charge such a device with an entire book relayed on-line from a publisher. It may well be the same publisher who has added the back-list to his data base as a prelude to one-off printing services. The book is then scrolled through on the screen and the reader sits back in his armchair to enjoy his 'book'. This does get over the resistance of many people to sitting in front of large screens all day long, although it is, of course, still a screen. It may be that brightness and stability of image will soon lead such devices to deliver a 'page' not materially different from a printed book. I have even seen a proposal that the text would be time rationed, in order to keep costs low, so that it had to be read in a certain time and not downloaded for future use or sharing.

Being somewhat old-fashioned in my book tastes, I find this package unalluring, but I will admit that it may well have a role in the future. I suppose it might also hold some interest for those worried by the future of the world's forests. Nevertheless, there are already signs that the price of printed books may fall to counteract this competition. If publishers were really convinced that this is the future, would they not be changing their production ideas now? There is plenty of evidence that even the smallest publishers are moving from computerisation into cyberspace, but largely to aid their sales of what one might call finite books. The delivery of academic information to students for specific purposes, often tailored in specific ways, may well become electronic, but any older bookseller will confirm that the day when students were major bookbuyers of anything outside the updated texts for their syllabuses are long gone. We have a minute sector of that market now and don't have much to lose. There will always be passionate booklovers, but they exist across the board, across classes and occupations. There is said to be a hundred-and-sixty-million-pound textbook market in this country, but little of it impinges on the used-book dealer – it takes at least fifty years for a textbook to move from outdated to collectible, as anyone trying to sell recent textbooks to general booksellers will rapidly find out to their dismay.

There may well be other developments as yet unforeseen, but the sheer utility of the printed book will take a great deal to supersede.

It is also useful to ponder what we are trying to sell. Make a list under the various headings, perhaps as follows:

- antiquarian and older books
- specialist subjects such as the arts or technical books where the books are bought partly for their expertise and partly for use
- modern first editions
- finely printed or private press books
- casual reading
- illustrated books of various kinds from older engraved plate books to modern etchings
- what I call back-up books, such as older travel books bought to flesh out the fine guide books now produced; and so on. One only has to categorise them to realise that remarkably few of them are susceptible to substitution. Even that

'casual reading' hardly seems to pose much of a threat.

I hope I am not simply conjuring up the arguments I wish to believe, a kind of whistling in the wind. I suspect that the next two or three years are going to see a considerable 'down-sizing' in the traditional new-book retail trade in the United Kingdom. This is not because the technology is turning against the printed book but because there has been drastic *over*-expansion in the past ten years. The rivalry between Waterstone's, Dillons and W.H. Smith was fuelled by a curious view that the overall market for new books was expanding fast, an idea which was always suspect. I do not know the overall figure for new-book sales now as compared to, say, the 1930s. The number of titles has vastly increased but I wonder how much the number of books sold has increased. With competing demands on time from TV, video and other mass entertainment, it might seem that the time available for reading has sharply decreased. I am not the only person who has noticed a contradiction in the statistics and some of the views built on them. Like the figures for illnesses, it may be that we simply collect the figures more efficiently these days.

Chapter IX

The Market and Entering It

SHORT-TERM PUBLISHING

The various fields explored in the first part of this book remain unaltered as we enter the new century but we have to look ahead, especially when building a business. Books are going out of print much faster, so we must value them more. If a book lasts nine months in the new market, six more if it is remaindered (and not everything is), then its price to those who want it may start to rise within a couple of years of initial publication. Many books are now printed in short runs and just because there are ten copies on the Internet does not mean they are necessarily common. On the other hand, those books of lasting value can be reprinted more easily now, which may undermine their secondhand value. If one-off printing does take off, the charge for it will effectively put a ceiling on the secondhand value of the original edition. This and the ubiquity of the Internet may mean that any rise in overall values will continue to lag behind inflation. It will be the exceptional used book (as usual excepting the first-edition market) which will be worth, say, more than one hundred and fifty per cent of the price of an average new hardback, but then that is already the case. Peter Eaton at his Lilies emporium used to display a notice as to the current average cost of a new non-fiction hardback book and most of his prices were always well below it.

The number of retail shops may have fallen, but there is no mistaking the public's goodwill to those that remain. Those who enter them may not buy all that much, but they love having them there. It is up to the bookseller to turn that appreciation into sales. Unfortunately, this is much easier said than done. Like many booksellers, I have often been disappointed that slashing the price of a book seems not to have the effect of selling it. Occasionally, putting the price up seems to have that effect! The retailer has to soldier on with his book fairs, his Internet sales, his catalogues and his window displays until persistence and familiarity pays off. Putting lots of books on the Internet, describing them properly and giving good service may well serve as a kind of super-advertising board for the shop itself. It is too early in the current revolution to know yet.

Where I have found that customers are price sensitive is in the specialist field. We sell most of our normal royalty books between twelve pounds fifty and twenty-five pounds, a price level that customers broadly accept as one which we need to set to run a viable business. Since we are the major buyers in the field, however, we are continually buying collections and we thereby accumulate large numbers of the more common titles in our field. Twice a year, winter and summer, we issue a sale list with perhaps two hundred and fifty royal titles reduced by around a third, usually books of which we have two or three copies. This has a marvellous effect, because we are selling to a captive audience who are already interested in the books and who may have been constrained before only by the shallowness of their pockets. The cuts must not be overdone, or customers will hold off buying full-price books in the hope of future cuts, as they now do with new books which may be remaindered. It does increase cash flow and eases some of the pressure on space from which we all suffer.

Even for the specialist, it is necessary to look constantly for new customers as others fall away. My main strategy in this direction has been to run a monthly magazine in the field so that word spreads through subscribers. It also, of course, has the beneficial effect of enabling me to charge for catalogues. Most booksellers will be unable to do this, but existing specialist magazines in the field must therefore be utilised. We even go as far as having a Royalty Weekend every spring at which fifty diehard collectors are given lectures, food and books in return for a modest fee. We now sell out every year and I am considering taking over the village hall to expand my numbers. Once they visit, they will not only buy books but they will be personally bonded into the business and its staff. At a more modest level, get-togethers of one sort or another, with perhaps a visiting expert or a well-known author, would not be so difficult to stage. Take a leaf from the more adventurous new bookshops, which have done this for years. Remember the book sessions for children in the film *You've Got Mail* ? – although, come to think of it, they didn't save her shop.

THE PERILS OF ADVERTISING

I have done as much duff advertising as the next bookseller, probably more. To achieve any real impact, display advertising costs big money. To spend even a hundred or two on a one-off display advertisement almost anywhere is almost always money wasted. If you must, a running small advertisement on the drip theory is much better and certainly much cheaper. Cheaper still is to develop techniques of getting into the editorial matter of your local newspaper or magazine. If you do anything worthwhile, buy something good or have almost anything interesting to say, either write to your local paper or send a press release. Many of them are quite pressed to find text to keep their advertisements apart. One word of caution here, however: be very careful how you publicise coups locally, for you do not want to start a whispering campaign that you swindle people who sell to you.

I have in my time taken significant space in attractive mediums like *The Times Literary Supplement* but it has hardly ever paid off. Small advertisements for customers for your catalogues may help, but not display advertising. I took a half-page once to advertise my shop and it included a voucher valid for six months giving a twenty-five per cent discount for one visit. We had two takers, one of whom said he had been planning to come anyway. If you have a really good specialist magazine for your specialist subject, by all means push the boat out and follow one large advertisement with a small box in every issue, but do not try to preach to the converted.

The lesson of the book fair is that booksellers do best when they take their books to places where there are customers. Outside Charing Cross Road and perhaps the centres of Oxford and Cambridge, book fairs are almost the only places where this is possible. I hope that the two trade associations will continue to reinvent themselves and their book fairs every so often in the next few years, for they will need to do so. The PBFA, probably the largest book fairs organisation in the world, has shown some signs of stagnation recently, with its flagship fair at the Russell Hotel threatened and some of the minor provincial fairs showing returns which make one wonder how long they can last. The ABA's two provincial fairs, Bath and Edinburgh, are both fairly marginal, although the strength of the Olympia Fair and the Chelsea one in the autumn are proverbial. I hope, although I am not entirely confident, that members of both organisations will continue to support the fairs and not think that the Internet replaces them. We still have to find books to sell and the knitting together role of the fairs must never be underestimated.

THE IMPORTANT BOOKSELLER

I have sometimes been criticised for blowing my own trumpet, writing too many articles and pushing myself forward in the trade. It might be said that the very book you are reading comes under this heading. I plead very guilty to this and I intend to go on offending. In your own way, you should do so too. A high profile is simply a relatively cheap way of publicising your business. I have always been proud to be a bookseller, which I consider something very special. Why hide your light under a bushel if you are in fact doing something you feel proud to be doing?

Read Boswell's diaries to discover how our brethren were esteemed in the eighteenth century. To be a good bookseller, you must needs cultivate your mind and this must enrich your general life. There can be no mistaking the interest shown by many people at parties when one says what one does. It may be that the average commuter is jealous of someone in an occupation like ours. He does not know the financial risks involved, the long hours, the unloading at book fairs on frosty mornings, the driving when one is over-tired, but so what! If he or she likes meeting and talking to a bookseller, take the opportunity to do a little of that trumpet-blowing. We are essentially a low-turnover business without the margins to devote to publicity, so we must be our own publicists. It helps to believe in what you are publicising.

My father, a Lloyds underwriter all his life, never quite rid himself of the idea that I would have been more respectable as a broker in the City than in a trade. He might have compromised on publishing and he pulled a string or two to get me my temporary stint at Longmans. Towards the end, he did try to overcome his old-fashioned prejudice, but he never quite succeeded. I, on the other hand, had a somewhat Dickensian view of the City and, in spite of an uncle who was one of the most successful insurance men of his generation, thought that insurance was a version of betting and that bookselling was a much more interesting occupation. I do not find it difficult to hold somewhat contradictory views of this trade – I think that it is a trade, that it obeys most of the same rules as other trades (I even criticise my fellows who shy away from the idea of the 'journeyman bookseller' and insist that it is a profession) but I do think of it as an intellectual occupation, calling for an interesting mind and a meticulous curiosity. Before one can convince customers or colleagues that one is a conscientious and potentially worthwhile bookseller, one must surely believe it oneself.

This is beginning to sound like an improving Victorian tract, so I will move on. I hope I have made it clear that I believe that the good bookseller is one who believes in himself or herself, who thinks laterally and is constantly looking for new ways to get through to a difficult, diverse and very small public. It may be that the Internet will uncover a vast new public for secondhand books, but there is no particular reason to think it will. Its main use will be to put you in touch with a much higher proportion of the public that does exist. Where there may be a minor breakthrough is with people who have in the past found the milieu of bookshops intimidating. It is the existence of those people, and I believe there are significant numbers of them, that makes it so important that book descriptions be understandable to the layman. We must not talk down to those feeling their way into their role as customers, a failing too many of us have been guilty of in the past.

A FINITE MARKET

It used to be said that under ten per cent of the general public ever crossed the threshold of a bookshop, new or secondhand. On gloomy days, we would downgrade the estimate to five per cent. The total market for the broadsheet newspapers is under four million in a population of sixty million or so. I doubt whether more than two hundred thousand people have *ever* opened a copy of *The Times Literary Supplement*. Yet there are over five million copies of Harry Potter books in print in this country now, so there is some room for expansion if we get the right product. Despite that startling fact and assuming that my proposition that the printed book will survive is correct, we will always be catering to a tiny minority of the population. Fortunately, there are only a small number of booksellers competing for a share of this small market. Within a reasonable distance, it is perfectly possible to know all of them and most of the committed customers as well.

The reason I make this point is that newcomers to the trade are often quite unrealistic about the parameters of the used-book field. For some years I sold books in Tavistock Market in Devon every Friday. A very significant proportion of all those who shopped there looked at my stall and I did indeed sell a lot of books. It gave me an idea as to possible markets which was quite unrealistic. I was selling very cheap books in a crowded market to a quite educated public, many of them retired professional people. Once I added the proper overheads of a shop, the picture changed completely.

I now sell books in an affluent village, but I cannot compete on paperbacks and more popular books with charity jumble sales, so I don't try. I could fill acres of shelving with paperbacks at twenty pence each and sell lots of them, but I couldn't pay the rates out of that, let alone wages and rent. Yet to most casual shoppers, secondhand paperbacks at a pound or more each are far too expensive. We have great big windows for display and this regularly draws people in to ask the price of some of the better books we display – tell many of them a price like twenty pounds and you would think they had been stung.

I think the new means of selling books will expand the market – slightly. A few more percentage points, however, will make a great difference to us. With most city or shopping-centre shops denied us on grounds of cost, it may well be that the great passing trade of the Internet will be the salvation of the small bookshop or even the dealer from home. This promise is already attracting many very amateur dealers into the field. Hence the importance of proper standards in dealing with customers, for reputation in even such a disparate space as the Internet will reap its rewards in terms of customers.

Chapter X

The Internet and Other Advances

SITES ARE BUSTING OUT ALL OVER

This is not, of course, an instruction book on how to enter the Internet. I shall assume that you already have your computer, that you are on-line and that you are aware of at least some of the host of Internet sites that seem to be daily hawking their services to booksellers. The cost per month seems to most of us extremely reasonable, more particularly because the comparison is in some ways with rental property. The temptation is to site yourself on too many of them, for each is only a few pounds monthly. It does all add up, however, and it seems to me far more important to choose the biggest site in the price bracket that interests you and concentrate on building up your presence on that one site. It is not that easy to build a presence, at least not one to the standards I have been advocating.

It is also quite expensive. What many dealers seem to do is simply buy a load of books or utilise an existing stock, catalogue everything in sight and slam it on to their chosen site. Some of the numbers one sees are quite startling. I was looking at one only today which listed well over twenty thousand titles. One wonders how much time that all took and what sort of return it all yields. It may be that the bookseller concerned has been on-line for years and that his present number simply represents a stock of, say, five thousand left from a past total of twenty thousand or so, since it is unusual to re-use numbers. Presumably such a bookseller is actually an on-line bookseller only, although the physical space and organisation required for such a stock is quite formidable. Before I started, I did monitor one or two major stocks in America. In each case I found that the movement of stock was very slight, or perhaps the owner simply neglected to remove sold items over long periods. I assumed that the dealers I was following did not have retail shops, since my own experience has been that retail customers seem to have a perverse habit of buying the books shortly after one has listed them and put them back on the shelf.

THE ROUTINE OF CHECKING STOCK

I trust that, as promised, British Telecom will be overhauling its price for on-line access around the time this book is published. At present, access costs a surprising amount, for the brief time needed to load your listings is by no means the end of the access needed. I have found that taking a shelf of books from stock and checking it against, let us say, the listings on ABE takes a considerable time. Yet it is just as pointless to list a copy of a common book at an unrealistic price on the Internet as it is to house it on a retail shelf. My own system is to check each title to find what other offerings there are. One rapidly forms a view of whether the book is going to be worth listing. If the search reveals that there is 'no match found' then matters are fairly straightforward – just catalogue the book in the normal way (unless it strikes you as valuable, in which case it behoves you to check its value elsewhere).

It is when you get a number of existing entries that you have to build some form of assessment. If the figure is above thirty, simply check the first batch to see how many of the copies match yours in edition and binding.

If several do and the price is low, it is probably not worth wasting your time adding it to the list. If most of them seem to be in poor condition, or in paperback, or late editions, one should persevere and even print down the list if required. On any long list, most of the listings will be in America or Australia, and I have found that it is often worth duplicating these for the UK market. Home buyers prefer home sellers, partly for the convenience and partly for the comeback in case something goes wrong. For this reason, incidentally, it is usually worth adding the initials ABA or PBFA to your name to inspire confidence. Even with a book with thirty listings, you may well find that only two or three seem to be UK, hardback, well described and within a competitive distance of what you had thought of charging. Ideally, of course, you should then undercut them, but do not do this at your own expense. If the book seems to you to be worth a certain amount, charge that even if there are some slightly cheaper books on the site. This method of assessment is time consuming and somewhat fiddly, but it soon becomes routine.

Pay some attention to your terms of trade. There are booksellers who do not take credit cards, but I think this effectively cuts them off from international sales. The site providers will normally help with such details, although other conditions depend upon you. Both of the main trade associations have rules about accepting returns and you should adhere to these even if you do not belong. I myself offer books post free in this country and add a flat three pounds per parcel outside the country, but most other booksellers add postage.

The credit card companies now fulfil the role that customer accounts used to occupy and this is a great convenience, since it means that we are becoming effectively a cash trade. One caution, however: just clearing the credit-card transaction with Visa or

Mastercard or Amex does not guarantee it. That guarantee number does not stop the customer cancelling the transaction at any time up to six months and getting the credit-card provider to retrieve the money from you, virtually for no reason. If you doubt this, ask your credit-card company about it. Remember, that guarantee number or even a direct-line machine provides no guarantee. It simply means the customer has the funds available at that moment.

Trade or institutional customers should be allowed thirty days' credit if requested provided you can certify that they are genuine from a reference book of some kind. Anyone else who refuses to provide either a credit-card number or send a cheque in advance should be treated with suspicion. One must, I think, respect the rights of people who refuse to use credit cards on principle, but they should be prepared to provide some other form of advance payment. I do not accept dollar cheques, as mentioned in my notes on credit in my first section, because of the costs of conversion.

UP-MARKET SITES

There are a few worthwhile sites other than ABE, although they are expanding so rapidly that I do not intend to name any. I think this is a field in which advice from fellow members of the trade should be sought. I do not like sites like Alibris which aspire to act as principals rather than as conduits. By this I mean that they offer you facilities to advertise books but it is they who sell them after marking them up. They buy them from you on behalf of the customer and sell them on. Although they take more responsibility for payments, they also keep the customer's name from you and you may also find yourself in the ludicrous position of advertising the same book at two different prices on two different sites. Whichever commercial site you do patronise, keep an eye on their conditions of sale, since such sites can change hands and the new owners may not be as straightforward or scrupulous as the previous owners. Sites like Biblion are attractive to various people, although they have price limits (or had) and their policies are geared to some extent to those people who display books in their West End premises. As far as I know, there has not yet been a guide published to book web sites, although I suspect this is only a matter of time. When it does come, let us hope it provides a detailed review of what facilities are offered, the background of those running the sites and what vetting procedures are carried out on dealers offering books.

Both the ABA and the PBFA are currently setting up sites geared to the needs of their particular members. I suspect that within a few months I will add both of them to my own sites, partly because I feel a considerable loyalty to both. The main reason each is exploring what is a fairly expensive option is that there is a widespread feeling in the trade that commercial sites have their own agenda and are in almost all cases vulnerable either to takeover or to financial instability. In each case, the trade associa-tion will limit participation to its own members, although in the case of the ABA this will include members of all affiliated International League associa-tions around the world.

The ABA is furthest ahead and is likely to have its site up and running by October 2000. Membership of the ABA is, of course, harder to attain, being restricted to full-time booksellers of five years' standing who have survived a fairly rigorous election test. The site is likely to be considerably up-market of ABE, but it will have considerable advantages. It will carry the full set of ABA rules as a kind of guarantee, with the possibility of ABA arbitration in the event of unresolved disputes between buyers and sellers. As far as I know, this proviso is not offered anywhere else yet. As I write, it already appears that a significant proportion of ILAB members from around the world will sign up to it and it is likely to provide 'hot links' to any other ILAB-approved sites around the world.

The PBFA, as is its custom, has concentrated on raising the money required first and is only now looking at the technical side. I suspect that its site will, when it takes off, be technically competent and its higher membership will ensure a fair spread of books offered. It is likely, like the ABA, to be protected from future takeover and the two sites together may well offer the best long-term future for booksellers with serious standards.

Some of the foregoing may sound unduly cautious and protective in a field distinguished for its unabashed openness. All I can say is that the bookdealer wishing to build a serious business must shy away from the Internet in its guise as a kind of Wild West of cyberspace. It may be fun to surf or to read about, but it is not something to build a business around or entrust with your future livelihood. I would expect that the next two or three years are going to see increasing interference in its workings by authority, either national or international. It is hard, when one seriously considers the subject, to think that this will be a bad thing. The net is already an avenue for major fraud, not to mention the threat of viruses and other technical dangers. I would suspect that the dangers are going to become more numerous rather than fewer. At its lowest level, the potential for tax evasion is such that something will eventually need to be done – we all dislike paying taxes, but states need financing and are hardly likely to take kindly to a form of international trading which is entirely unsupervised.

PUBLISHING AS A SIDELINE

I hope Chapter VIII indicated that developments in publishing are as much subject to technical innovation as any other part of the book field. Assuming that the printed book does survive, its production will continue to become cheaper and more flexible. I believe that booksellers should capitalise on this. As I have remarked, it is now possible to reprint books for relatively modest prices in very small quantities. Technology enables the reprinting of existing books and the creation of new books where authors provide text on discs or CDs with ease. In the former, apart from choosing the materials and binding style, scanning in text and proofreading totals the practical chores, but, of course, compliance with copyright laws must be observed. New titles usually require some editing, checks for libel and inconsistent style, but other than these there is little difference, and there are nowadays plenty of expert freelancers around to help.

Booksellers should pay more attention to this possible ancillary activity. The retail bookseller should look at local options. Assuming there are no restrictions on copyright, he can reprint small editions of his locality's topographical works or books by past authors with local connections. If there is no good local guide, he should produce one which can be sold either exclusively in his shop or retailed around the locality. There is usually a local historian who can produce the text on disc and is often pleased to do so for either a straight fee or a royalty. The former is preferable, since then you will own the text and can go on reprinting as needed without paying extra in fees. If the local work has other connotations, the bookseller might well be able to find another specialist bookseller to take half of a small edition and share the cost. It has often been said that the real problem with secondhand bookselling is that, when you find something that sells, you cannot lift the telephone and order more. Publishing in modest quantities at least gets over that problem.

Likewise with the specialist bookseller. At a very early stage the specialist will discover a fair quantity of titles sought, often desperately, by his burgeoning list of customers. The only problem is that he cannot find them. A modest programme of putting at least some of them back into print need not cost a fortune and adds another dimension to his reputation and to his cash flow. I myself have some thirty-six titles on royalty in print at present, editions varying from fifty to five hundred copies. I have plans for more. My reprinting programme has been a considerable success, although I suspect that this is partly because I have, unlike with my previous venture in the early 1970s, remained small and not been seduced into thinking that, with my small resources, I can produce books suitable for the general new-book trade. If the specialist bookseller is effectively the only source for various titles, persons interested in his subject will beat a path to his door, which is surely to be welcomed.

REVERTING TO OLDER PRACTICES

It is sad that more booksellers do not take the time to study the history of their trade. There has been a steady trickle of books on the history of bookselling in recent years, associated largely with the name of Robin Myers, the archivist of the Stationers' Company. Many have been published by St Paul's Bibliographies, which is now owned by Oak Knoll Books. The various biographies associated with members of the family of John Murray, older works like Knight's *Shadows of the Old Booksellers* and sundry autobiographies of nineteenth-century booksellers are all of interest.

The reason why I mention this at the end of a chapter on modern technical innovations is that I think one can learn from the past. As the modern publishers amalgamate, their financial strength is vastly increased but so is their vulnerability. They cannot *afford* to pursue many of the projects the trade and the public would appreciate. If you go back to the beginning of the nineteenth century, you find that many books were published by groups of booksellers in various cities who effectively took shares in a new publication. With the new technologies available now, it might well be possible for groups of dealers, whether new or secondhand, to revive this practice so that, say, either a reprint or an original work could be printed in a run of two or three thousand copies and then broken up between ten booksellers spread around the country. They could be available from no one else.

There have been various essays published containing studies of the various things booksellers used to sell in the eighteenth century, from medicines to stationery via practically everything else. I would not advocate this: in fact, in my experience even excursions into cards, prints and other vaguely allied fields often end badly. Either the bookseller moves into full-time dealing in prints or he finds that the new stock takes up more space than its turnover justifies. I have tried combining bookselling and coffee-bars myself but it never really worked. Nevertheless, the twenty-first century bookseller should always be on the lookout for something allied to his basic trade that might work. Bookbinding has been in decline in recent years, and the incorporation of a bookbinder into a retail shop could benefit both trades – if the binder were prepared to work in public view, so much the better. I have no doubt that there are other opportunities which have not occurred to me, or even innovations which may develop in the next few years which could be adapted to our trade. It is closed minds that are at a disadvantage these days.

Two points arise from the previous paragraph which merit a diversion. The first concerns bookbinding. You may well find a bookbinder who suits you and who, without going into partnership with you, will bind for your business. Inevitably, after a little, customers will ask you to get their books bound for them. Beware of this. I know, for I have past experience of being piggy in the middle between a binder and a customer. It is simply not worth any margin you may be able to make on it. Things go wrong far too often and it is the middleman who gets the blame.

I enjoyed my excursion into running a bookshop-cum-coffee-bar. During one of my broke periods when I went part time, I worked in London during the coffee-bar craze of the early 1960s. When I went back into bookselling, I decided to put this experience to use and I started a coffee-bar-cum-bookshop in Reading. The coffee-bar side went reasonably well, but the bookshop was a washout. There was hardly any carry-over from one to the other. We had customers who took coffee with us for months without realising we sold books, despite being surrounded by them. There are bookshop *habitués* and there are coffee drinkers. Sometimes they coalesce in the same person, but that happens naturally. You cannot force-feed people something alien to them.

The other obvious way of sharing overheads is to share a shop with a number of other booksellers. It has been practised in recent years with varying success in Bath, Ludlow, Dorchester, Hay-on-Wye, Greenwich and London (in Long Acre and Great Russell Street) to name those that spring to my mind. The very up-market Biblion in the West End I have already mentioned. My own, Baggins, is slightly different in that the books are completely fused in subject rather than dealer sections. On the whole, the experiment has been fairly short-lived. It spreads the rent and rates and, if the booksellers run the place in turns, it cuts out wages, but it is somewhat impersonal and the resulting shop does not have the ambience or build up the local goodwill of a shop owned and operated by one business. I counsel caution.

The great advantage of the Internet is that it does allow dealers to operate wherever they like, even in places where the only passers-by are sheep. For small provincial retailers, it may well offer the extra dimension that enables them to survive. I think that, for most booksellers, it will, at least for the next few years, need to be combined with other outlets, be they book fairs or e-mailed catalogues. Specialist bookdealers may well be fated to end up as specialist web sites, with perhaps personal photographs and 'editorial' to add humanity to the screen presence.

One consideration must be borne in mind, however, and it is an important one which has, I think, been overlooked by those proselytising for the Wigtown experiment in Scotland. There are two sides to dealing in used books – buying and selling. The selling side can be skilfully adapted to the Internet, but the buying can be only marginally relevant. One should, of course, buy such specialist books as one can find on the Internet for one's own stock, but buying books in proper quantities still means getting around looking at likely places to find books, attending auctions, frequenting shops of various kinds and buying privately. Settle in a remote (if cheap) area and one narrows one's horizons in almost all of these endeavours. However efficient one gets at selling one's stock by the new technical means, whatever all-singing-and-dancing web sites you may devise, you must have the books to sell first. Hay-on-Wye, remote as it may seem when you are there, is within fifty miles or so of several major conurbations: Wigtown is not. Before you settle into your rural paradise, with your accumulated book stock bought in lunch hours in the city and your computer at the ready, think on that.

Chapter XI

Bureaucracy and Other Matters

SMALL TRADERS AND TAXATION

As we get further into this century, it is very clear that not only are trading habits going to change but the tempo of change is going to accelerate, and anyone intending to start a permanent business needs to look ahead. In the past two years, for instance, the liabilities taken on by anyone setting out to employ people have increased substantially. A serious book-dealer is going to have to employ someone, even if it is only a packer or a part-time shop assistant. Part-timers are acquiring more rights: even getting rid of a part-time packer who is unsatisfactory is getting more difficult. The new laws were simply not devised for small businesses who may be 'employing' people whose main object is having something to do rather than earning significant sums. The increase in total awards for wrongful dismissal from twelve thousand to fifty thousand pounds represents, in itself, a substantial potential liability, for employment tribunals are notoriously tilted in favour of the employee. In most cases, solicitors will suggest any action be settled out of court, however innocent the erstwhile employer may be.

On the other hand, tax paperwork for those with turnovers below two hundred and fifty thousand pounds has decreased significantly. For those with alternative income – and I have stated that alternative income is very desirable in the early stages of a second career – initial losses can be offset against tax and this is now very easy. Small businesses which are not companies no longer have to return detailed accounts, although these must be available for inspection if required. The net profit or loss simply has to be entered on one's tax self-assessment form and either added to or subtracted from one's total income as appropriate. For someone with a significant pension or rental income, this can be a considerable help in setting up a bookselling business.

As of now, bookselling continues to be a zero-rated field for VAT purposes. Unless you are in it at a very basic level, it is essential to register for VAT since this allows significant claims for VAT to be repaid. My present business in Ticehurst averages around twelve hundred pounds in repayments per quarter and this covers all my accounting costs with something to spare. I fully expect, however, that if this book runs to future editions I will eventually be dealing with the effects of a European-imposed change, even at a relatively low rate. This has been fought off for the present.

STOCK VALUATION

The matter of valuing a book stock is always a tricky one. I know at least one bookseller who built up a major stock through the years on the basis of a rock-hard stock item of just a thousand pounds. It is notoriously easy to build up stock, but most back stock will be books one has failed to sell within a certain time. While there will still be an element of unrealised profit in most of it, much of it will consist of mistakes and one does not wish to value it too highly. In bulk, quantities of back stock have a very low value on a forced-sale basis.

At least in the early stages, few of the books concerned will have been bought on a single-book basis. If you paid twenty pounds for a book and have priced it at forty pounds, it should naturally go into any stock valuation at cost, i.e. twenty pounds. In most other businesses, it would be proper to depreciate it over a period but this is very debatable with second-hand or antiquarian books. This straightforward method will only apply to a small element of your stock, however – most will have been purchased in lots. Some people go solemnly through and assign a purchase price to every item, in the shape of codes inside the book or entries in a stock book. I really think this is a waste of time with cheap books. Say you pay seventy-five pounds for three boxes of cheapish books brought into your shop, perhaps a hundred books in all. To say that each book has cost seventy-five pence is ridiculous. Purchases simply do not work like that. Carry the estimate done in the purchasing over into your (imaginary) valuation. You have almost certainly paid sixty pounds for ten books, which you will price up to, say, a hundred and fifty pounds or more. The other ninety books have been lumped in for fifteen pounds and they may well gross up to another hundred and fifty pounds, but the work involved in dealing with them mops up a lot of this cost and, in any case, they may well end up as background stock, present on your shelves for years or even sold on in bulk to someone else at auction. To put them into any overall valuation of your stock at (say) forty per cent of the hundred and fifty pounds they have written inside them will be to create a paper profit which may be both awkward and unrealisable. By extension, this creates a considerable problem as your stock gets larger. The problem has never been resolved for this type of business and my solution has always been to estimate a total.

For the medium-sized general secondhand stock, work out what the *absolute minimum* is that you would take for it if some besotted buyer came in and offered to buy the lot. Put that in.

When you move up in the world, it may well be possible to estimate a good deal more accurately. With a good speciality and a stock where most of the books have been bought individually, it may even be possible to evaluate a stock completely accurately, especially if the whole stock is listed on computer and the entry includes what it cost you.

This may be of some use to you later should you ever wish to sell the business. That curious phrase 'with stock at valuation' means something with a new-book stock, although even there the purchase price will need to be depreciated for staleness. With secondhand books, most purchasers will not be prepared to work on a figure of what you have priced the books at, less an agreed percentage. If, twenty years down the road, your stock is running at a thousand hand-picked books with a proven figure of twenty-five thousand pounds as their purchase price and a marked-up 'value' of fifty-five thousand pounds, allowing for a fair number of sleepers you might reasonably expect to charge thirty-five to forty thousand pounds to a purchaser of the business. I use this simply as an example when discussing valuations. In fact, as I will mention in my concluding chapter, such a stock would need to be a specialist one being sold on to another specialist to achieve this kind of result. The 'normal' way of selling on a good general stock will be either in small parcels at a fixed discount or at auction.

For the present, it is useful to give some thought to the matter of valuing your stock before you go anywhere near an accountant. Most professionals are not used to dealing with stocks of this kind where a book is largely 'worth' what the seller says it is worth. The only area of your stock which might be worth depreciating over a period is any reprints or remainders in which you may have invested. Once you have creamed the market, the residue of these would certainly have a small book value on a forced-sale basis. Valuable specialist businesses also tend to carry their reference libraries at a fairly high valuation, but here again reference works are prone to date. To take an example, I have a great run of *Book Auction Records*. The later volumes cost me something like eighty pounds each. It is now easy to pick up copies of most volumes around the twenty-pound mark and once the whole run has been listed free on the Internet I suppose the set will have hardly any value at all. In theory, they should stand in my accounts at several hundred pounds, whereas, in fact, they should be depreciated and the sums involved knocked off my profits.

Fixtures and fittings are easier to depreciate and most accountants know and apply the normal rules regarding this. Curiously enough, practically nothing has been written in the trade on the question of second-hand-book yearly accounts, even in the normally informative columns of *Bookdealer*. I don't know whether this is because bookdealers are secretive about their accounts and their profits. I have written the odd article or two on it in *Antiquarian Book Monthly* and the *ABA Newsletter*, but there has been virtually no feedback. Yet getting it right may not only ease one's own worries but also sometimes be of material help in the early stages of a business. Booksellers should share their experiences, since getting serious professional advice can be a costly affair and may be a futile one given the unusual problems which arise in our particular business.

REFERENCE BOOKS

I mentioned reference books above. I would imagine that much of what I would have said on this a couple of years ago is now out of date. For your specialisation, if you have one, the key books will rapidly become apparent. Runs of past catalogues in your field, while perhaps outdated on pricing, are invaluable on description. The general bookseller, unless he is a great reader himself, should beware of piling up too many so-called reference books which should really be in his or her stock. The basic tools will increasingly be available either on the Internet or on CD-Rom. The key reference work is now the Internet listings themselves, as I indicated in the previous chapter.

Where I think many booksellers fall down is in the field of general knowledge. I have the reputation of being a bookseller who reads books, a fact reflected in the ABA committee's presentation to me of a reading stand when I retired as their president, a choice that pleased me greatly. The aim is for the customer to *think* you have read the book you are trying to sell. You won't have, of course, but a little experience and a deal of *blague* can leave him uncertain on the point. Background reading is essential. If you are recommending a biography and then make it evident that you know absolutely nothing about the person whose life you are selling, it sounds tacky. If you are ignorant on the matter, admit it. If you have to make such admissions too often, do something about it. Older dealers making a second career in bookselling have an advantage here and they should exploit it. A nice line in mildly literate chat should be cultivated, although this should not be forced on unwilling listeners. It can also be carried to extremes. Driff, the former writer of guides to booksellers, used to go on about booksellers who pursue you round the shop talking at you. There is a delicate mean to be achieved here.

There are, of course, author bibliographies which must be to hand should you wish to make any kind of speciality in their subject. The *National Dictionary of Biography* and its various supplements is always useful. There are also some excellent biographical dictionaries now available for more modern authors and a run of *Who Was Who* is helpful. Dealers will find their own level. My basic advice would be to keep it under control – reference books are expensive and some of the money on your reference shelves might be better deployed turning over in your business. A fifty pound reference book used once a year may be a bad buy, especially if it is available in a public library or in the ABA library.

Perhaps I should say a word about remainders. By this I mean the remains of runs offered by publishers or remainder wholesalers at reduced prices. There are a number of these wholesalers – Sandpiper, Powell in America, Roy Bloom and others. They are very good at sending out lists, although they almost all have a minimum order of fifty or a hundred pounds nowadays. One gets a third off the listed price and that price is frequently only twenty per cent or so of the original recommended price. To anyone devoted to books, the lists are very beguiling. There is also a whole floor of remainder dealers at the annual Olympia New-Book Fair in the spring and other specialist remainder fairs are promoted from time to time in the trade press.

If you are a specialist bookseller, you must look through these lists and buy up a small number of anything directly in your field. General retail dealers can also often find remarkable bargains and occasionally even local books they have overlooked. To reap the maximum reward from remainders, however, it is best to sit on them for some time. There are specialist remainder shops out there which will be selling the title at the recommended price, say a twenty-pound book at four pounds ninety-nine. If the book is a good book, your aim should be to sell the twenty or thirty copies you buy at fifteen pounds a copy but to do this you must wait until the remainder shops have run out. It won't be long. Then sell your copies at the higher price over a long period. The investment usually pays off.

MORE HERESY ON BINDING

I have dealt briefly with binding before, but I would like to emphasise the benefits of finding a reasonable cloth binder and sticking with him. As the new-book trade becomes more and more orientated to paperback production, hardbacks in newly re-bound condition become more attractive. Many booksellers turn their noses up at re-bound books, but my customers don't. This is one of those areas where past prejudices still cloud the judgement of the trade. I have a prejudice against throwing good titles away simply because they have poor covers. A reasonable cloth binding (or new case as it is sometimes known) can often be added for ten pounds or less, especially if your binder gets a fair amount of work from you. This will turn an impossible book into a reasonable proposition at twenty pounds or so and have the subsidiary benefit of saving a decent book for the future.

I used to get a lot of leather rebinding done, but this has become too expensive for most of the books I want to save. At least in the early stages, you do not want to have too many volumes on your shelves with sixty or seventy pounds wrapped up in the binding, let alone the cost of the book. Even with good leather binding or rebacking, books become harder to sell in non-contemporary condition as you move up the price scale. A couple of shelves can easily tie up several thousand pounds for far too long.

I don't do it myself, but I have known several booksellers who do their own minor repairs. It is probably a good idea to go on a course to learn this, for a capacity to tidy up labels, put in new endpapers and even effect repairs on the outside of books can save lots of money. If you can progress to actual binding, this could prove an interesting sideline but it is almost certainly not cost-effective. If you can make more money bookbinding from a given two or three hours than you can bookselling, then become a bookbinder.

BASIC DESCRIPTION

One of the major changes which the expansion of bookselling into a more general marketplace will achieve is, I am convinced, a simplification of book descriptions. I am now going to catalogue three books chosen from my own personal shelves more or less at random and then make a few comments on what I have written.

Magazine: THE BOOKWORM. An Illustrated Treasury of Old-Time Literature. Octavo, 420 pages plus frontispiece and title-page, line-drawings in text, new cloth, quarter brown with green sides, fore and bottom edges untrimmed, small Grimsby Library stamps on several pages (not particularly obtrusive). London: Elliot Stock. 1888

Warburg (Frederic): AN OCCUPATION FOR GENTLE-MEN [Publishing]. Octavo, 288 pages, illustrated, purple cloth; no dust wrapper. Very good. London: Hutchinson. 1959

Mumby (Frank A.): THE ROMANCE OF BOOKSELLING: A History from the Earliest Times to the Twentieth Century. With a Bibliography by W. H. Peet. Octavo, xviii & 491 pages, numerous illustrations, original red cloth decorated gilt, untrimmed; rebacked, with original spine relaid. Tight, clean copy. Bibliography runs to 39 pages. London: Chapman and Hall. 1910

This is pretty basic cataloguing, but it helps me make a point or two. There are some slight variations in size between the three, but too technical to note; they are all what a normal customer would recognise as octavo. The first item should really have [iv] before the pagination figure, but I don't think people understand that, so I describe the two extra pages. To me, 'untrimmed' means not guillotined flat, whereas 'uncut' means that the connected-up pages have not been slit with a paper-knife. I now add 'London' since that is what the Internet people like. We used to preface a catalogue by stating, 'unless noted, all books published in London'. I now note when a modern book (*vide* #2) does not have a dust wrapper, since we get queries about this nowadays. I have also added [Publishing] to that item, since the title is not self-explanatory. If either of the other two *did* have a dust wrapper, I would make a major mention of it. I mention the length of the bibliography in the last item, since it seems to me to be a selling point.

It will be noticed that there is not a single abbreviation in those three basic examples. On the whole, I think we should now be moving away from complicated abbreviations and writing things clearly. If we want to tap into a larger market comprising people with different backgrounds, from each other as well as from us, we will have to compromise. Many booksellers' catalogues are still written for classically educated book lovers, as are those scholarly works

that do not translate Greek, Latin, French or German
quotations into English, and I simply do not find that
acceptable any more.

Chapter XII

Tying It All Up

The original suggested title for this last chapter was
'How to Close Down Your Business' but I simply
cannot bring myself to fit in with that particular
constraint. I will, however, start by trying to address
it.

Let us say you have either built up your business
over a number of years or bought somebody else's
business and run it for some time. You decide to
finish your second career and retire properly or
decamp to Ibiza for some sun. Nine times out of ten,
in my experience, used-book businesses finish themselves rather than get wound down in a systematic
way. Either the lease runs out or the owner dies. In
many cases the owner simply runs his activities down
as he gets older. It is very difficult, once you have
frequented jumble sales, book fairs or other shops for
a number of years, simply to stop. One just fades out.
There is a retired list at the end of the *ABA
Yearbook*, but it is really very small and many of
the people on it are either booksellers' assistants or
widows who cannot bear to cut their links with the
trade.

Where a retail bookshop does close down, it
normally ends in one of three ways. If the bookseller
owns the property, he sells it for something else, for
the sad fact is that the property is very often worth
much more without the bookshop than with it. Sad,
but true. He then sells off the fixtures and fittings and
has a prolonged sale of the books, finally selling the
balance off to one of the brokers' men (often either
Richard Booth or myself). As often as not, he has

taken a few books home and he continues to buy and sell from there until he dies, but in a modest way. It is the freehold money that is important.

The second option applies to someone who may have a fairly large shop with a good lease. If the lease is too good, it will again be worth more than the business. If not, he has to find someone to buy the business from him as a going concern. This is going to take time and effort and will almost certainly mean his taking a much reduced price for the stock. In almost all cases, he will have stopped investing in stock some time before, so what he has to offer is 'tired'. In only a few cases, of which the only recent example that springs to mind is Titles of Oxford, will he find a significant customer, and in the case of Titles that was largely because the business had a good name and was in an excellent position in Oxford. If you are looking ahead ten or twenty years and do not own a freehold, my advice would be to invest in a good retirement policy now or buy an extra house on a mortgage elsewhere and let it. I cannot in all conscience say that retail bookshops have in recent years been bankable propositions from the goodwill viewpoint.

The third option is sadder still and unfortunately more common. The bookseller simply removes himself and his residual stock to his home so that he can go on doing book fairs and lists until he drops. He then sells off his fixtures and fittings and such stock as he does not want and hopes that what he realises pays for the dilapidations at the end of his lease. End of story.

The last three paragraphs should really, of course, be treated as a supplement to my Chapter 3, 'Retail If You Must'.

The specialist bookseller is, I think, in a somewhat better position. If he has built up his stock properly, with a wide-ranging coverage, good reference books, a proper customer list, sound reputation and a lasting subject, he has something *portable* to sell. His immediate customers may be his rivals, if he has any. Rather than approach them direct, a hint dropped here and there could be more productive. If that fails, he can advertise the business in the book-trade press or, perhaps better, in the specialist magazines of his speciality. This may attract the attention of someone else with the same interest and a desire to sell books in that field. A geologist close to early retirement, for instance, might consider selling geology books from home and consider an offer an easy way in. The whole business can then be removed to the buyer's home, perhaps after a training period, and the seller is free to pursue whatever other interests he may have from his own home.

There are, I suppose, gradations between these various extremes, but the main point is that there are really only four elements in any bookselling business, except perhaps at the very top end: there is the owner's expertise, the property, the stock and the goodwill. Of these, the owner is the one who is selling, the property I have dealt with above, the stock, unless it is a fine specialist stock, is unlikely to be worth a great deal and the goodwill is a very variable element. Given a significant sum of capital, the prospective purchaser might just as well invest it in books of his own choice and simply set up in business. It is difficult to see wherein any extra value lies.

KEEPING OPTIONS OPEN

Let us leave that depressing subject and try to sum up where I see this trade headed. The innovations are on balance positive. The Internet offers a major market place to anyone anywhere and thereby removes the major problem of recent years, that which states that you cannot sell enough books retail except in a key position and the trade can no longer sustain the rents in key positions. The intense competition which will result will perhaps lead to some downward movement in prices, except with scarce books, but then we may, by checking the Internet, discover more scarce books in surprising categories. The increase in potential buyers is the major plus point.

I think some of the mystique will leave the business and I find it difficult to be sorry for this. It has been apparent over the past thirty years that older books, say before 1800, were a diminishing market. I suppose the major bull market in books since the war was in steel-plate books, but that market became saturated and has quietened down. It has been replaced by the first-editions field, which seems to be the only field in which the 'new money' entrepreneurs now coming into the foreground are interested, if they are interested in anything in our field. It is just possible that, after a slow overall decline in the total used-book market since 1950, the new technologies may be sparking something of a turnround. One likes to think that the triumph of the viewer over the reader may be reversed through sheer boredom, but I am inclined to think that this is but wishful thinking.

Both of the British trade associations will, I think, rise to the new challenges, which is important in itself, since I am quite sure that the plethora of unpoliced web sites will confuse future collectors but that eventually some element of order and code of standards will have to be imposed in this and other fields. The chaos typical of the web at present has grown up in parallel with a culture of blame, where aggrieved customers reach for their lawyers at the faintest whiff of any real risk. These two cannot coexist. Both the ABA and the PBFA will have proper sites up and running within a year and I would recommend any serious beginner in this field to put his trust in one or both of them in the long run. At least some of the e-commerce sites will be but memories in a few years' time, whilst the mutuals of the trade associations will still be soldiering on.

The future of book fairs is more problematical. I think both associations will tend to concentrate on larger, very well-run fairs in the future, leaving much of the provinces to smaller operators. The small part-time stall selling everything from cheap books to postcards or other ephemera will doubtless continue and will be as rewarding to the casual customer as to the person running it. I think, however, that much of the serious buying will be through the Internet and this will be fiercely competitive.

The only flaw in this scenario is the matter of delivery. However efficient the net becomes, the books and other goods ordered over it still have to be delivered. It is already apparent that the delivery firms covering *private* addresses in both Britain and America are barely capable of handling the present level of sales, let alone any significant increase. The business-to-business side is fine, but delivering goods to private houses when all the inhabitants are out at work is a problem which is barely being addressed. The pundits predict a fourfold increase in Internet sales within the next fifteen years, so the problems can only get worse.

A FINAL MYSTERY

I mentioned at one point that private lots of any size are becoming scarce on the ground. We have had a number of years now when production in the British publishing industry has risen sharply, yet this has not reflected through into the supply of secondhand books.

It may be that most of the editions are small, that many relate to specialised fields and education, that junk paperbacks take up an undue quantity of the figures – I do not know, but I have had talks with a number of major new booksellers and they also sense a mystery here. The *Bookseller* reported recently that sixty per cent of all new-book sales stemmed from just five hundred titles of the one hundred thousand titles published in 1999. I would like to see more research into this phenomenon.

I cannot see much beyond the next two decades and even there the prospect grows misty. I am confident that the antiquarian and secondhand trade will still be around in 2020. I have mentioned an estimate that of the four thousand people in Great Britain, known to be concerned in this business, barely five hundred made a full living from it. Before the reader takes the decision to transfer from the three-thousand-five-hundred majority into the five-hundred minority, he or she may well have found something in these pages to make them think. If, despite all the caveats, you do make the jump, I hope you never regret it. I never have.